The British Museum

nosy crow

A HISTORY OF THE WORLD IN 25 CITIES

Written by
Tracey Turner and Andrew Donkin

Illustrated by
Libby VanderPloeg

For Toby Battersby, polyglot and all-round marvel.

T.T.

For Lexie Donkin, historian of the future.

A.D.

For my mom and dad, who handed me my first road atlas on one
of our many family road trips, spurring my fascination with maps,
and for Erik, my favorite person with whom to explore the world.

L.V.P

First published 2021 by Nosy Crow Ltd
The Crow's Nest, 14 Baden Place,
Crosby Row, London SE1 1YW
www.nosycrow.com

ISBN 978 1 78800 671 2

Published in collaboration with the British Museum.

Text © Tracey Turner and Andrew Donkin 2021
Illustrations © Libby VanderPloeg 2021

A CIP catalogue record for this book is available from the British Library.

Printed in Italy.
Papers used by Nosy Crow are made from wood
grown in sustainable forests.

3 5 7 9 8 6 4 2

CONTENTS

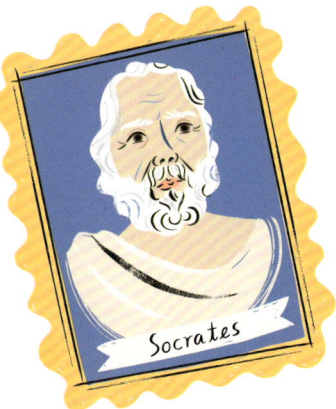

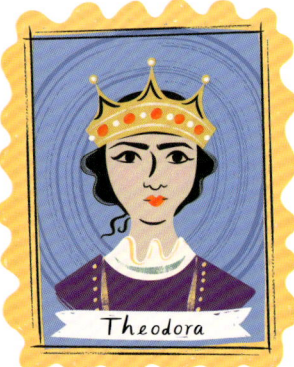

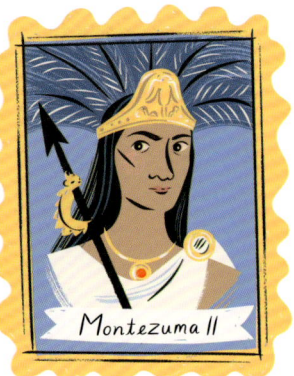

Socrates

Qin Shi Huangdi

Theodora

Oba Orhogbua

Montezuma II

CITIES

The Story of Human History

Cities are full of possibilities. They are where big ideas are born, because they welcome people from far and wide, bringing them together to live and work, and to swap skills, inventions and thoughts. We've been living in cities for thousands of years, and now more and more of us are choosing city life.

Together, the 25 cities in this book tell the history of human life. The first city we'll visit is Jericho in the Middle East, home to around 2,000 people over 10,000 years ago, when hardly any cities existed. The last is modern-day Tokyo in Japan, which has the highest population of any city on Earth today – more than 38 million people. Today, cities are home to more than half of all the people in the world.

All the cities we'll visit have fascinating stories to tell – of wars and revolutions, the rise and fall of powerful empires, and the movement of people all over the globe. Each of these cities is exciting and unique. Turn the pages and you'll be transported to Athens in ancient Greece, where the first democracy was born, Beijing at the time of the mighty Ming dynasty and Paris during the French Revolution, when rebellion brewed in its crowded slums. You'll find out what daily life was like for people in all of these very different places and times.

Some of these cities are thriving, bustling places today – many of the buildings from 2,000 years ago still stand in the modern city of Rome.

4

Others are in ruins, like Cuzco, the Inca capital city, or lost beneath desert sands, like Memphis in Egypt. Some are hidden within modern cities that have grown up on their ruins – the temples and pyramids of Tenochtitlán are hidden beneath modern Mexico City, and the beautiful palaces of China's first capital, Xianyang, have been destroyed. But you can step back in time and visit them in this book.

Read on and discover...

A mountain city full of palaces and temples, laid out in the shape of a puma.

A city of islands linked by bridges, with canals instead of streets.

A city deep in the rainforest, glittering with beautiful brass carvings.

A forbidden city, which no ordinary person could enter on pain of death.

We'll also look at what cities of the future might be like – perhaps they'll be built to encourage wildlife, using sustainable energy, with buildings alive with lush, green plants.

Get ready for a fantastic journey. Prepare to walk the streets of 25 amazing cities, on a voyage through human history, travelling across the centuries and around the world.

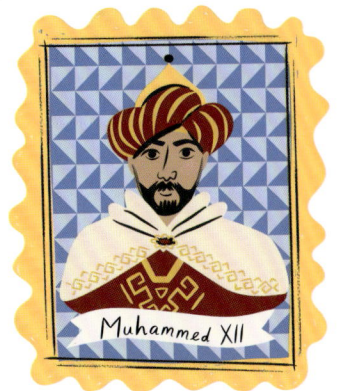

Muhammed XII

Bungaree

Marie-Antoinette

Queen Victoria

Zora Neale Hurston

JERICHO

Around 8500 BCE

Jericho, one of the oldest cities on Earth, lies in the Middle East. Before the first towns or cities, people travelled about and lived in small communities, hunting animals and gathering plants to eat. As people gradually learned to grow crops, farm animals and store their food, communities began to live together in one place, eventually forming towns and cities.

Tower

This tower might have been used as a lookout point. It was at least two storeys high and had 22 stone steps inside it. It's the oldest known staircase in the world.

Houses

The first houses in Jericho were built in about 10,000 BCE and were round and made of sun-dried clay and straw. About 1,500 years later, houses were rectangular and built of mud bricks, with stone foundations.

Courtyards

Rooms were arranged around courtyards where people made fires for cooking.

Walls

Walls around the city kept invaders out. The walls were rebuilt many times but the first ones, built in around 9000 BCE, are among the earliest city walls known in history.

6

Farming

Rich soil and a good supply of water meant people could grow crops like lentils, wheat and barley.

Spring Water

These natural water springs in and near the city meant that even though the surrounding land was very dry, the people of Jericho always had access to clean water for their families and herds of animals.

The Dead Sea
↙ 10 km Southwest

Being close to the salty Dead Sea meant that the people of Jericho could trade salt for other goods.

Jordan River Valley

Jericho lies in the valley of the River Jordan. At almost 260 metres below sea level, it's the lowest city in the world.

RIVER JORDAN

LIFE IN JERICHO

Jericho

WEST BANK

People have lived in Jericho for 12,000 years or more — longer than any other city on Earth — and there's still a city there today. But what was life like for families back in Jericho's earliest days?

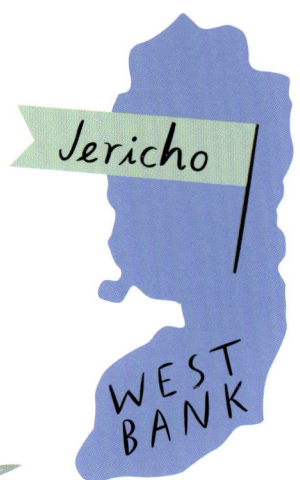

First Families

By about 10,000 years ago, houses in Jericho were built using sun-dried mud bricks. Most family life happened in the largest room in the house, while smaller rooms might have been used as bedrooms or for storage. People spun and wove cloth to make clothes and they used stone tools to harvest crops and kill animals. Living in a city meant that gradually different people could specialise in different jobs, becoming farmers, craftspeople, soldiers, priests or traders.

8

Burial Rites

The early people of Jericho usually buried their dead (sometimes even under the floors of their houses). In some cases the skulls were kept separately. Some skulls were covered in plaster to make life-like faces, using shells to represent the eyes. It's possible they were kept on display as a way of remembering what a family member had looked like after they were gone.

The Walls of Jericho

The people of Jericho built huge stone walls around the city and a lookout tower (at least 6,000 years before the pyramids of ancient Egypt were built) to keep themselves safe. The walls were rebuilt many times because of attacks, falling into disrepair and at least once due to an earthquake.

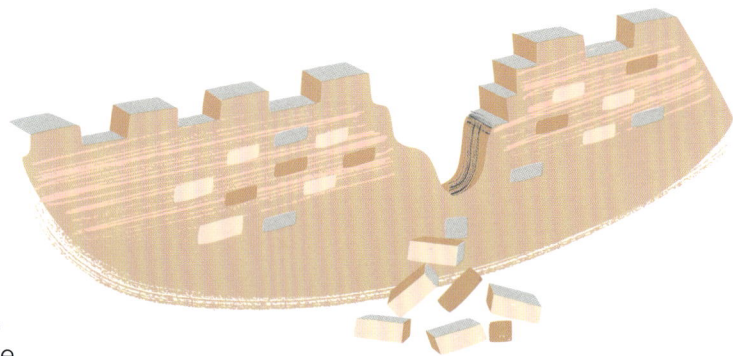

JERICHO IN NUMBERS

Number of times the walls of Jericho were rebuilt: **More than 20**

Time since people first lived in Jericho: **At least 12,000 years**

Children 9,000 Years Ago

During the first few thousand years of Jericho's existence, there was no written language. There were no schools and no teachers. Children learned everything from the people they lived with. It seems that some babies had their heads tightly wrapped up in order to change the shape of their head as they grew up. We know this from several of the skulls found but we don't know exactly why they did it. Perhaps they thought it made them look good!

A Very Long History

10,000 BCE
The first people settle in Jericho.

8500 BCE
People are building sun-dried mud brick houses and making plastered skulls.

1900–1550 BCE
The Bronze Age: chariot-riding Canaanites arrive and settle in the city.

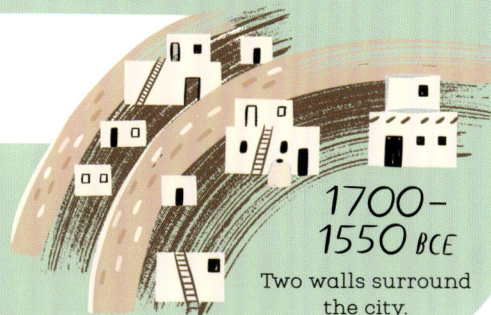

1700–1550 BCE
Two walls surround the city.

1550 BCE
Jericho is destroyed by an earthquake.

700 BCE
The Assyrians are in charge of Jericho, followed by the Persians and the Romans.

600s CE
Jericho is part of the Islamic Empire.

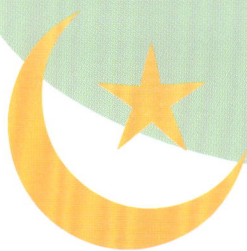

1500–1900s
Ancient Jericho gets less and less significant.

Today
The modern city of Jericho stands about two kilometres away from the ancient city, in the state of Palestine.

Population of ancient Jericho in 8500 BCE: *About* **2,000**

Population of Jericho today: **20,000**

MEMPHIS

Founded as the new capital when Upper and Lower Egypt became one, Memphis remained the largest and most important city in Egypt for 3,000 years. Originally known as *Inbu-Hedj* or 'White Walls', because its painted mud brick palace shone brightly across the desert, Memphis was a city of workshops and warehouses and was said to be under the protection of the god Ptah, the patron of craftsmen.

Stepped Pyramid of Djoser

Built around 2650 BCE to the northwest of Memphis, this was the burial place of the pharaoh.

Saqqara, the Necropolis

Warehouses

This vast burial ground housed many tombs, temples and pyramids. *Necropolis* means 'city of the dead'.

← 20 km North

Pyramid Power in Giza

The three largest pyramids in Egypt are near Giza, 20 kilometres north of Memphis. They were built around 2500 BCE and took thousands of workers decades to build. The largest, called the Great Pyramid, was built from over two million stone blocks. All three pyramids were finished in bright white limestone and had a golden cap at their summit. Standing guard was the famous Sphinx, a huge statue carved out of stone to look like the head of a human on the body of a lion.

Canal System

Designed for transport and protection, this network of waterways also provided water to grow crops.

Desert Edge

Out in the barren desert were gold mines.

Workshops

10

Cult Palace of Apries

Dedicated to the worship of the Apis bull, believed to be the living form of the god Ptah. Inside, a ceremonial bull was cared for by priests. After death, it was mummified and a new bull was chosen.

Sacred Precinct of the Temple of Ptah

These high stone walls protected the temple, which could be accessed through five enormous gates.

Great Temple of Ptah

The largest and the most important temple in the city. Located in the city centre, this temple enjoyed royal patronage from Ramesses II, later known as 'Ramesses the Great'.

Cult Palace and Embalming House of Apis

Alabaster Sphinx

Temple of Ramesses II

A small temple dedicated to Ramesses II. It included a large pillared hall, a tower and an open courtyard for rituals.

House of a Million Years of Ramesses II

Colossal Statue of Ramesses II

A huge 14-metre-high statue carved from a single block of granite.

Palace of Merenptah

A stone temple alongside a large ceremonial palace.

Wooden Barges

Trading ships were built of wood. They were propelled by both sail and oars.

RIVER NILE

The Nile is the second longest river in the world.

11

LIFE IN MEMPHIS

For thousands of years, Memphis was the largest and most important city in Egypt. But, rather strangely, during its long history the city actually moved location! Parts of the city were abandoned, and new areas built as the mighty River Nile changed its course and gradually drifted eastwards. The city of Memphis no longer exists today. Much of its remains lie hidden beneath several small modern villages that have sprung up where the mighty trading city once stood.

Family Life

The family was the most important part of ancient Egyptian society, and most boys were married by 18 and girls by around 14 years of age. Unlike many other societies at the time, men and women had almost equal status, and it is thought that some girls, as well as boys, might have been taught to read hieroglyphs, the pictorial symbols that make up the written ancient Egyptian language.

Memphis

EGYPT

The Majestic Nile

Along with the rest of Egypt, Memphis depended on the River Nile for fresh water for people to drink, as well as water for growing crops. The river flooded every July, leaving behind it very rich, fertile farming land. The Nile was also used as an easy way of transporting people and goods, although you had to watch out for aggressive hippos and hungry crocodiles.

A Trading Nation

Egyptians swapped their goods for what they wanted from other traders. Merchants from Memphis traded with many other countries in the Middle East to the east and in Africa to the south, as well as sailing across the Mediterranean Sea. Memphis was one of the richest cities in the ancient world, partly because of the gold mines located in the desert to the east that kept wealth flowing into the city.

The Rule of Pharaohs

The pharaoh was the absolute ruler of Egypt, and he (or, very rarely, she) set the laws, collected taxes, owned all of the land, and was responsible for keeping the people safe from war and invaders. Pharaohs were seen as god-like beings, and often married their siblings or half-siblings to keep the bloodline 'pure'. Pharaohs often had many children, with Ramesses II recorded as having 156 children!

Gods and Goddesses

The Egyptians believed in over 2,000 gods and goddesses, many of which were shown as half-human, half-animal beings. The most important god was the sun god, Ra.

Egyptians believed that every dusk, Ra was swallowed by the sky goddess, Nut, as it went dark. Ra spent the night travelling through the underworld so he could be reborn at dawn. Each Egyptian home had its own little shrine to the gods, where the family would worship daily.

Life After Death

Egyptians believed that by preserving the body of someone who had died, they could ensure that person's soul would live on in the afterlife. They did this through a process called mummification, in which the person's internal organs (apart from the heart) were removed. The body was coated with salt and left to dry for 40 days before it was stuffed and wrapped in bandages.

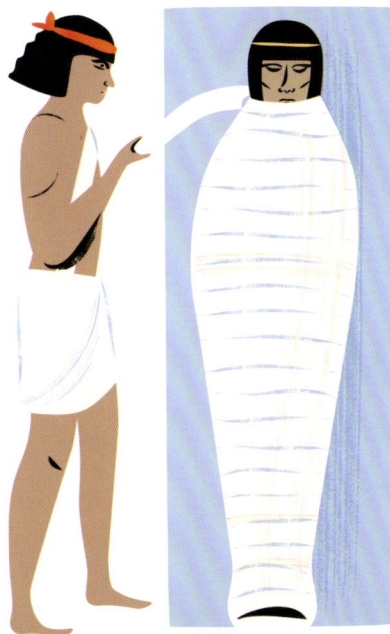

MEMPHIS IN NUMBERS

Number of pharaohs who ruled Egypt:
About
170

Length of time Memphis existed:
3,500 years

Population of Memphis around 1200 BCE:
30,000

Population of Memphis today:
0

ATHENS

In the ancient Greek world, cities and the areas around them were small, independent regions, or city states. During the sixth and fifth centuries BCE, Athens was one of the richest and most powerful of them all. Around 2,500 years ago, the ancient Athenians developed a new way of running things, giving every male citizen the chance to have their say. The Athenians had invented democracy.

Acropolis

This hill overlooking Athens was called the Acropolis, or 'high city'.

ILISSOS RIVER

Statue of Athena

Daughter of Zeus, the king of the gods, Athena was the goddess of war and protector of Athens.

Farmland

Athens was rich because the land was good for farming and there were marble quarries and silver mines nearby.

14

Parthenon

Inside this temple was a 12-metre-tall gold and ivory statue of the goddess Athena. Athens was named after her.

←

Odeon

Aegean Sea
9 km Southwest ↗

Theatres

The Theatre of Dionysus could seat 25,000 people.

Areopagus

A hill of bare marble used as a meeting place.

Pnyx

Athenian citizens gathered on this hill for political meetings.

Mint

Silver coins were made at the mint.

Council of 500

Athens' government met here.

Agora

People met here to trade and talk. There were shops, temples and public buildings.

Temples

Temple of Hephaistos and Athena

Not all Athens' temples were on the Acropolis. Hephaistos was the blacksmith god of fire and volcanoes.

Law Courts

Shaded Walkways

People met and chatted here. Philosophers talked about the meaning of life.

ERIDANOS RIVER

LIFE IN ATHENS

The city of Athens has existed for thousands of years. Back in the 'Golden Age' of Athens in the 400s BCE, city life was very different from how it is today . . .

GREECE
Athens

Rights for Some, Not for All

You could only become a citizen and take part in the running of Athens if you were a man, and not a foreigner or an enslaved person, so even though it was one of the first democracies, it was not a very equal one. Most women in ancient Athens couldn't take part in politics, own property, or even go out on their own if they were from a wealthy family.

Between a quarter and a third of the people who lived in Athens were enslaved people. They included policemen, servants and workers on farms or in mines and quarries. You might be born into slavery or be captured in war. Enslaved people didn't have any rights and their owners had complete control over their lives.

16

Gods and Goddesses

The ancient Greeks worshipped a lot of gods and goddesses. The most important ones were supposed to live on Mount Olympus, a high mountain a long way north of Athens. Here are just a few of them:

Zeus
chief god

Hera
chief goddess

Aphrodite
goddess of love

Apollo
god of the sun

Poseidon
god of the sea

Athena
goddess of wisdom and war

Hades
god of the underworld

ATHENS IN NUMBERS

Tonnes of marble needed to build the Parthenon: *About*

100,000

Number of Athenian citizens: *About*

30,000

Girls and Boys

In wealthy households, young girls and boys lived with their mothers in the women's quarters, separate from the men. Children's toys included swings, see-saws and yo-yos.

At the age of seven, well-off boys were sent to school to learn maths, reading and writing, sport and music. Girls didn't go to school – they stayed at home and learned how to spin, weave, sew and look after children. Boys of poorer households didn't go to school either – instead they went to work with their parents, along with the girls.

Young men aged 18 were given two years of military training. Athens was often at war, and every citizen aged between 20 and 50 could be called on to fight in battles or patrol Athens' borders.

WHAT'S IN A NAME?

In ancient Athens, a girl might be named Lysimache or Syeris, while a boy might be called Stephanos or Theomnestos. But in daily life, girls and women were hardly ever called by their actual names. Instead, they were often referred to as the daughter, wife or sister of a man in their family.

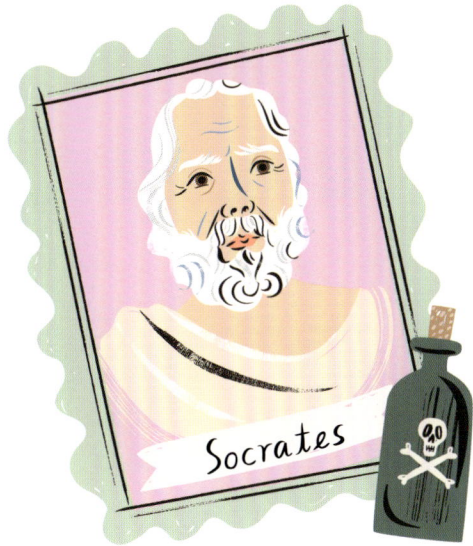

HELLO
my name is
Lysimache

Socrates

★ FAMOUS FACE ★

While all the hard work was being done by enslaved people, some Athenians had time for thinking and writing.

The son of a stonemason and a midwife, Socrates became one of the most famous philosophers in history. Unfortunately for him, some people didn't like his ideas. He was accused of corrupting young people and sentenced to death by poison.

Greek soldier

Spartan soldier

The End of an Era

Athens was at war with the Persians for 50 years (the Greeks won), and for 25 years against another Greek city state, Sparta. Sparta won that war, in 404 BCE, and Athens was never as powerful again.

Population of Athens city (including foreigners, women, children and enslaved people):

About **300,000**

Population of Athens and the surrounding area today:

3.75 million

XIANYANG

212 BCE

Ancient China was made up of independent states that were often at war with each other, until Qin Shi Huangdi united China into one country for the first time in 221 BCE. He became China's first emperor and made the city of Xianyang his magnificent capital.

Royal Library

Inside Xianyang Palace was the city library. The emperor was the only person allowed to have copies of 'forbidden' books – written before he came to power. All other books were burned.

Xianyang Palace

Bronze Statues

These statues were made from the weapons of the emperor's fallen enemies, or possibly from weapons taken from the people of Xianyang to prevent a rebellion.

Palaces

These represented the defeated states and housed trophies.

Luxury Homes

These palaces were built for the rich families that Qin Shi Huangdi brought with him to fill his capital.

Workshops, Markets and Homes

Outside the Xianyang Palace walls, the city was a bustling hive of activity.

Xin Palace

The emperor's palace.

Great Hall

This huge building could fit up to 10,000 people inside.

Sweet Springs Palace

The emperor built this palace for his mother, Queen Dowager Zhao.

Epang Palace

This enormous building site was to become the emperor's new home.

900 km North ↑

To stop invaders, Qin Shi Huangdi joined up many earlier walls to form a version of the Great Wall 5,000 kilometres long.

New Highways

Part of a huge new road network across the empire. The central section was reserved for the emperor's black imperial chariots.

The Emperor's Tomb

Building began when Qin Shi Huangdi was 13 years old. It included a huge palace for the emperor in the afterlife.

19

An Army of Statues

Many thousands of labourers, most of whom were probably enslaved, crafted and painted this lifelike terracotta army made of 8,000 warriors. There were also terracotta servants, entertainers and court officials — all destined to accompany the emperor to the afterlife.

WEI

RIVER

Farmland

Rich green land surrounded the city.

Buried Treasure

Chariots pulled by four bronze horses were found buried here.

Li Mountains

XIANYANG IN NUMBERS

Area of tomb:

170
square metres

Number of figures in the terracotta army:

More than

8,000
warriors,

150
cavalry horses

and 130
chariots

Population of Xianyang in 212 BCE:

600,000

Population of Xi'an today:

835,000

LIFE IN XIANYANG

Little remains of the magnificent palaces of China's first ever capital city. But hidden in the ground, an army made of terracotta and a unique, pyramid-shaped tomb reveal a glimpse into life in ancient China more than 2,000 years ago.

Life in the First Empire

Emperor Qin Shi Huangdi lived in a huge, luxurious palace. Wealthy noble families lived in beautiful houses and palaces too, although many of them had been forced to move to Xianyang by the emperor to fill his new city, whether they wanted to or not.

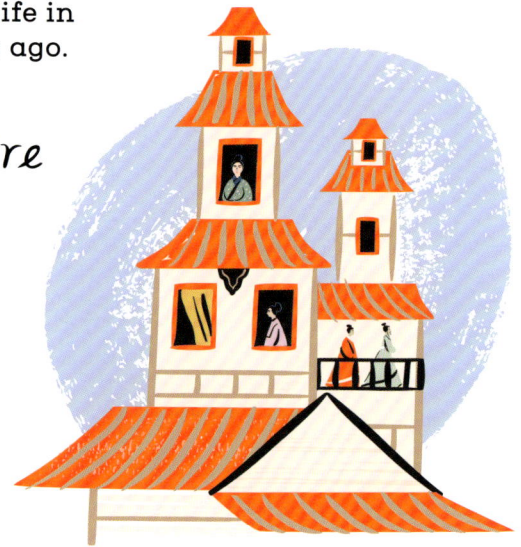

Rich citizens were the only people allowed to wear silk – even silk-sellers weren't allowed to wear it. Men and women of all classes wore their hair long, pinned or tied up, because they believed hair came from their ancestors, and to cut it would be disrespectful.

CHINA | Xianyang

Less wealthy people might have been warriors in the imperial army, merchants, or some of the many officials who kept the empire running smoothly, but most people worked as poor farmers, silk harvesters, or were set to work building roads, canals or the first Great Wall of China.

The Tomb of the First Emperor

Qin Shi Huangdi died in 210 BCE. No one knows exactly what lies inside his enormous, pyramid-shaped tomb, but it's thought to contain an exact copy of the imperial palace he lived in when he was alive, its ceilings painted with constellations of stars. It's possible the tomb is protected by traps for tomb raiders, such as archers that fire real arrows if the tomb is broken into.

Terracotta Army

The emperor had a life-size clay army made to protect his tomb and serve him in the afterlife, made up of thousands of painted warriors, chariots and horses. Also discovered were painted terracotta archers and even entertainers such as acrobats and strongmen. The statues were buried and forgotten for centuries, until farmers rediscovered them in 1974.

★ FAMOUS FACE ★

Qin Shi Huangdi became ruler of Qin when he was just 13. In nine violent years, he conquered the six states that surrounded his own to create his vast empire in 221 BCE. He made weights, measures and money the same throughout China, employed officials to make sure it ran smoothly, and put up monuments that declared the country was unified and he was in charge.

Qin Shi Huangdi

End of an Era

The Qin dynasty only lasted 15 years. The Han dynasty took over, burned down Xianyang and moved their capital to Chang'an. Both cities are now part of the wider area of the modern Chinese city of Xi'an.

ROME

100–200 CE

The city of Rome in Italy ruled a powerful empire that stretched from the deserts of Africa to cold northern Britain. Known as the 'capital of the world', it was the most important city in the Mediterranean for over a thousand years.

Food and goods were transported along the great River Tiber. The river also carried away the city's sewage.

RIVER TIBER

Pantheon

This enormous domed building was dedicated to the worship of all the Roman gods.

Theatre of Pompey

Tablinum

Rome's record hall.

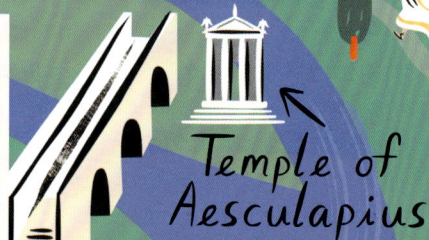

Temple of Apollo

Capitoline Hill

Temple of Vespasian

Temple of Jupiter the Best and Greatest

Generals came here to thank the god Jupiter for victory in battle.

Temple of Aesculapius

Servian Wall

Fire! Fire!

Rome was a very crowded city with many dangers on its unevenly paved streets. The city watchmen doubled up as Rome's fire brigade and every household was required by law to keep firefighting equipment – such was the danger of fire in the densely packed city.

Public Latrines

There were no private cubicles in public toilets, and people used a communal sponge on a stick instead of toilet paper.

Trajan's Column

Aqua Marcia

Rome couldn't have grown so big without the clean water brought by its aqueducts. They were marvels of engineering, sloping very gently to provide a constant flow of fresh water.

Temple of the Divine Julius

Julius Caesar was worshipped as a god after his death.

Trajan's Market

Temple of Venus and Roma

Subura

Rome's roughest neighbourhood.

Trajan's Baths

Roman baths were more like modern leisure centres but on a much bigger scale. People would meet here for business and to socialise.

Forum

This area of the city was the centre of Roman politics, religion and law.

Arch of Titus

This was a monument to a Roman victory.

Colossus

A 30-metre high statue of the Roman sun god, Sol.

Temple of Vesta

The 'sacred flame' of the city of Rome burned here, guarded by priestesses who made sure that it never went out.

Imperial Palace

The emperor's home.

Palatine Hill

The grandest houses in Rome were built here before most of the neighbourhood was covered by the imperial palace. We get the word 'palace' from 'Palatine'.

Colosseum

Gladiatorial fights, animal hunts and executions all took place here.

Nero's Golden House

The Emperor Nero's vast palace.

Circus Maximus

This chariot racing track could hold 250,000 spectators. The emperor could watch a race from the palace, or from his imperial box, which was connected to the palace by a private walkway.

LIFE IN ROME

Almost 2,000 years ago, Rome was the largest city in existence. It included magnificent public buildings and grand palaces, as well as busy shops, market stalls and blocks of flats several storeys high.

Rome

ITALY

Kings and Emperors

At first, Rome was ruled by kings, then governed by elected officials. Augustus Caesar became the first emperor in 27 BCE – although he called himself the 'first citizen' of Rome instead.

Rich House, Poor House

Houses for the very wealthy had impressive entrance halls and up to four luxurious dining rooms where lavish feasts were served to guests who ate lying down on low couches. These grand houses also had running water, private bathrooms, ornate gardens and underfloor heating. Poorer people lived in blocks of flats three to five storeys high, often with shops on the ground floor. They had no kitchens and bought their hot meals from food stalls in the streets. Flats could be crowded, noisy and rat-infested, and some were so badly built they collapsed.

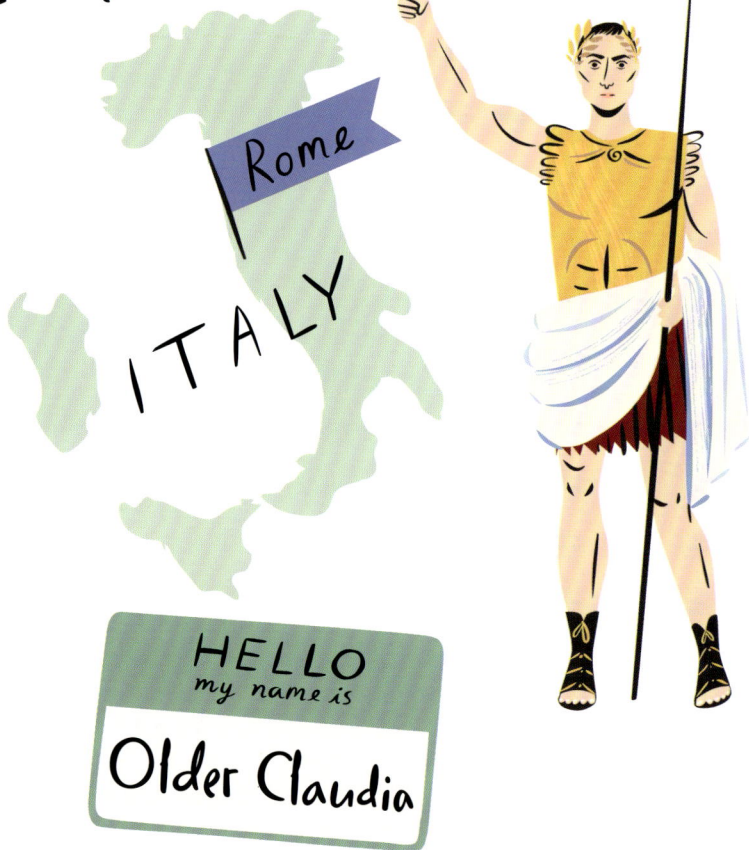

WHAT'S IN A NAME?

Your name told everyone your status – whether you were freeborn or had been enslaved. Boys usually had a first name – often Gaius, Lucius or Marcus – plus a clan name and a family name if they were Roman citizens. Girls were often only given female forms of the clan and family names. Common clan names were Claudia and Flavia. If there were several girls in one family, they might be called Older Claudia, Younger Claudia and Third Claudia.

ROME IN NUMBERS

Size of Empire at its biggest in 117:

More than **5** million square kilometres

Size of the Roman army:

300,000

★ FAMOUS FACE ★

Hadrian became emperor in 117 CE, when the empire was the biggest it would ever be. The vast empire was difficult to control – Hadrian gave up some of it and built defences to protect what was left, including Hadrian's Wall in northern Britain to keep the fearsome Caledonians (modern-day Scots) at bay.

Hadrian

Gods and Goddesses

As well as the many gods the Romans borrowed from the Greeks, there were gods of the household and all sorts of others, from a god of doorways to a goddess of sewers. Roman life was full of festivals, rituals and sacrifices because there were so many gods to keep happy. The winter festival honouring the god Saturn involved presents and feasts, a bit like Christmas, and masters and their servants swapped roles for a day. As well as festivals, there were many rituals, including animal sacrifices, after which priests would look at the animal's insides to predict the future.

Built by Enslaved People

Rome relied on its population of enslaved workers, who might have been captured by the army or have been born into slavery. Enslaved people had a wide variety of jobs, as accountants, shop assistants, teachers, household servants and lots more. Some were gladiators, who fought to the death in the Colosseum – the successful ones became famous, and sometimes free men and women fought as gladiators hoping for fame and fortune. Enslaved people could be freed by their masters, and sometimes they earned enough money to buy their freedom.

The End of an Era

The Roman Empire split into two halves in the 300s, the eastern half ruled from Constantinople (modern-day Istanbul). Rome was attacked and defeated by invading tribes in the 400s, and much of it fell into ruin for centuries.

THE ROMAN EMPIRE

Population of Rome in 100s: About 1 million

Population of Rome today: About 2.8 million

CONSTANTINOPLE

Originally called Byzantium, the city was renamed Constantinople in 330 CE to honour Emperor Constantine, who made the city the new capital of the Eastern Roman Empire. Constantinople became one of the biggest and wealthiest cities in the world, shining with gold, bronze and polished marble.

500s CE

Palace of Blachernae

The emperor's second house.

Senate House

The centre of government.

Constantinian Wall

Built on the orders of Emperor Constantine, the wall surrounded the city.

LYCUS RIVER

Theodosian Walls

Less than 100 years after the Constantinian Wall was built, a new double-wall, separated by ditches and moats, increased the size of the city and protected it from invasion.

26

Mese

The 'middle' or main street of Constantinople. It was 25 metres wide and lined with colonnades (covered walkways) and shops.

Forum of Constantine

This wide, circular meeting place housed the Column of Constantine, with the emperor's statue at the top.

Golden Gate

This grand entrance to the city was covered in marble statues, bronzes and gold decorations and was used only on special occasions.

Sea Walls

Marble Tower

The Theodosian Walls had towers for defence.

SEA OF

Golden Horn

Early settlers believed this inlet of the Bosphorus looked like a deer horn.

EAST meets WEST

Constantinople stands on the border between Europe and Asia, the only city in the world to straddle both continents.

Bosphorus

This narrow stretch of sea separates Europe from Asia.

Hagia Irene

The first Christian church in the city.

Monastery of Stoudios

Obelisk of Thutmose III

Emperor Theodosius brought the obelisk from Egypt in 390.

Hippodrome

An arena for chariot races that held more than 60,000 spectators.

Hagia Sophia

This beautiful church was famous for its high and wide dome, which still stands today.

Baths of Zeuxippus

Public baths decorated with beautiful mosaics, where people would meet and talk as well as bathe.

Great Palace

Next to the emperor's throne were two golden lions that actually roared, while mechanical birds sang from a golden tree.

Lighthouse

The lighthouse helped to guide ships in and out of the city's busy harbour.

MARMARA

LIFE IN
CONSTANTINOPLE

In the middle of the 500s, under Emperor Justinian, Constantinople was one of the world's richest cities. Hundreds of thousands of people lived there, from many different countries and cultures.

Constantinople

TURKEY

A Divided Empire

The Roman Empire had split into two halves: the Western Empire, ruled from Rome, and the Eastern, or Byzantine, Empire, with Constantinople as its capital. In 476, Rome was taken over by invaders, ending the Western Empire, but the Byzantine Empire continued for hundreds of years. Taxes raised from the empire made Constantinople rich; it was full of palaces, churches and public buildings, many built from marble and decorated with gold and bronze. The city traded and grew richer still, and its busy streets were full of shoppers, merchants and luxurious goods such as silk, spices and incense.

Blues Against Greens

People in Constantinople were big fans of their favourite sport: chariot racing. The sport was so important that a passageway led directly from the emperor's palace to his seat in the arena. The two teams, the Greens and the Blues, were deadly rivals and there were often fierce fights between them. But then the Blues and the Greens united in an attempt to overthrow Emperor Justinian, and around 30,000 people were killed when they failed.

Christian Rivals

Back in the 320s, Emperor Constantine had been Rome's first Christian emperor. But by the time of Emperor Justinian, the Christian Church had started to split into two branches: the Catholic Church and the Eastern Orthodox Church. Eventually, the two religions became completely separate, and they still are today.

★ FAMOUS FACE ★

Theodora was the wife of Emperor Justinian, and a remarkable woman. Most emperors' wives were royal themselves, but Theodora was born in a circus. Her mother might have been an acrobat, and Theodora had married and had children with a bear-keeper who died young, and was already married for a second time when she met Justinian. She changed laws to make things better for women – divorce laws, property laws and laws to punish violence against women – and helped Justinian conquer and govern the growing empire.

Theodora

WHAT'S IN A NAME?

Constantinople was a cosmopolitan city. People came from all over Europe and Asia to live and work there, so names came from lots of different cultures – Benjamin, Leo, Joseph, Alaric, Anastasia, Maria, Brunhild and Theodora might all have met in Constantinople. Both boys and girls from wealthy families would have gone to school, at least until secondary school.

The End of an Era

Constantinople survived as the capital of the Byzantine Empire for over a thousand years, protected by its strong walls. Eventually, the city was taken over by the Ottoman Empire, after being invaded in 1453. Now called Istanbul, it's the modern Republic of Turkey's largest city, where you can still see the Hagia Sophia, the Column of Constantine and many other remains of its Byzantine past.

Column of Constantine

CONSTANTINOPLE IN NUMBERS

Population of Constantinople in the 500s:

500,000

Population of Istanbul today:

15 million

Size of Constantinople:

6 square kilometres

Size of Istanbul today:

1,539 square kilometres

BAGHDAD

Baghdad was founded when the Abbasid ruler, Caliph Al-Mansur, moved the capital of the Islamic world to the banks of the River Tigris in 762. Known as the 'Round City', it was laid out as a huge circle 2,700 metres in diameter. At the very centre was an area of gardens so beautiful that it was described as 'paradise on Earth'. The gardens contained the ruler's palace, a huge mosque and an impressive library. Developed over decades, Baghdad grew to become a great centre for culture and learning during what became known as the 'Islamic Golden Age'.

The House of Wisdom

This was a huge library. Its collection of books attracted scholars from all over the known world. Unfortunately, it was later destroyed, leaving its contents a mystery forever.

Houses

Homes were built from mud and brick. They usually had several rooms with a courtyard at the centre. Many included roof terraces and decorated balconies.

Mosque

This impressive mosque, which was connected to the palace, was situated at the very centre of the city. It was built by Caliph Al-Mansur.

Caliph's Palace

Home to the ruler of Baghdad, who was known as a caliph, a title given to the leader of the Muslim community.

Tea Rooms

Meeting places for business and pleasure.

Camel Caravans

Camel caravans brought people and goods across the desert. They often carried items to trade such as precious metals, salt, spices and leather.

Fortified City Wall

Built to defend the city, the wall kept Baghdad safe until 1258, when the city was captured and destroyed by the forces of the Mongol ruler, Hulagu.

30

RIVER TIGRIS

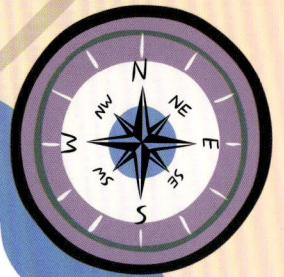

Hammams (Bathhouses)

The city's many hammams allowed people to stay clean and healthy, as well as being a place to meet friends and gossip.

City Gate

There were four huge city gates linked to the centre, called Syria, Kufa, Khurasan and Basra.

Trading

Baghdad's docks were large enough for hundreds of different ships to come and go at once. Trading vessels and their owners brought goods here from all over the known world.

Dhows

Ships called 'dhows' with a triangular sail carried goods and people all over the region, sailing between ports on the Persian Gulf and across the Indian Ocean as far as China.

Government Buildings

Flower Gardens

Beautifully designed with fountains and flowing water features.

31

City of Wisdom

Baghdad quickly established itself as a place of learning and science, with a constant flow of scholars and scientists into and out of the city. Central to this was the House of Wisdom, also known as the Grand Library of Baghdad. Manuscripts were brought here from far and wide to be translated into Arabic. This gathering of knowledge from other cultures led to many amazing discoveries in medicine, mathematics and astronomy.

Markets

Busy colourful markets sprang up around the city gates selling food, leather, jewellery, fabrics and carpets.

LIFE IN BAGHDAD

Baghdad was a cosmopolitan city where scholars of different faiths could study together. This freedom to debate resulted in many exciting advances in science. Doctors discovered new cures and drugs, including one that put patients to sleep during surgery. Before that discovery, all patients used to stay wide awake during operations! Scholars also invented algebra and the decimal system of nine numbers and a zero, now used everywhere in the world.

Baghdad

IRAQ

32

Changing the World

Some new inventions like the astrolabe had a profound effect on the world. The astrolabe was an intricate device that could be used to measure the positions of planets and stars in the sky. This meant you could tell exactly where you were on the Earth. It was especially important because it allowed Muslims to work out the direction of Mecca while travelling. In time, it would be used by European sailors to help navigate large distances across oceans.

Me and My Shadow

Theatre shows were very popular in Baghdad. However, instead of starring human actors, they were called 'shadow theatres' and featured shadows projected on to walls. The shows usually took place just after sunset and could be held anywhere in the city. The highly skilled puppeteers controlled the shadow puppets with long, thin rods attached to their moving parts. Shadows of the puppets were cast on to a large wall using a very bright lantern. Shows would attract large crowds, who enjoyed the stories into the evening.

BAGHDAD IN NUMBERS

Up to

Number of workers involved in the four-year construction of Baghdad:

100,000

Height of the city's outer defensive wall:

School's Out

Children in Golden Age Baghdad got a good education. Well, half of them did, at least. Boys were taught to a higher standard than girls, because it was expected that girls would stay at home doing domestic work when they were grown up. Most boys went to school at their local mosque, but if you had very rich parents, they might hire a private tutor to teach you at home. Pupils wrote in Arabic with ink made from soot.

Go with the Flow

The River Tigris gave the people of Baghdad access to lots of fresh water. Water wasn't only needed for drinking. It was also very important in growing food. The city's engineers built high-banked canals to carry water from the river to where the crops were grown in the fertile soil of the floodplain. The canals could act as defences too, making the city harder to invade. River water was also channelled into the city's flower gardens, where it flowed through fountains and beautiful pools.

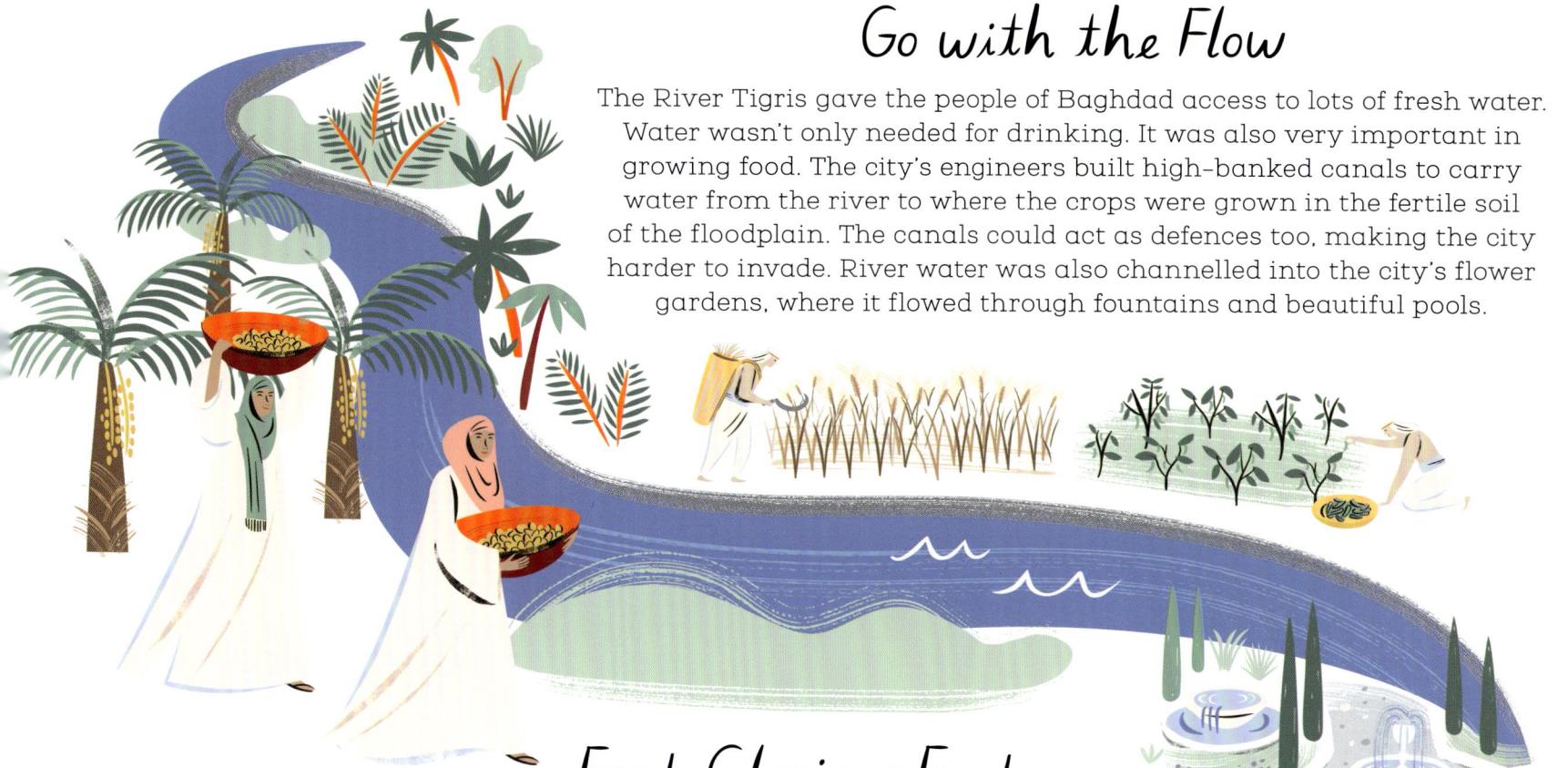

Food, Glorious Food

If you lived in Baghdad during the Golden Age, you probably had a pretty good diet. Advances in water management and farming meant that more food could be grown easily in and around the city. Residents enjoyed dried dates, honey, milk, figs, grapes, bread, and meat from sheep and goats. Food was also imported from faraway places, such as spices from India and fruits from Africa.

26 metres

About **1** million
Population of Baghdad in the 800s:

About **7** million
Population of Baghdad today:

JÓRVÍK

Jórvík in 940 was a growing city and a major trading port in the north of England. In 866, Vikings had invaded a large part of northern England, capturing the city that would become known as Jórvík and is today called York. Jórvík was a place where both Anglo-Saxons and Vikings could feel safe and at home. Although Jórvík was inland, it was connected to the North Sea by the River Ouse, so local craftspeople had access to the whole Viking trading network.

A route to the North Sea allowing traders to travel all over Europe and beyond.

RIVER OUSE

York Minster

Started life as a wooden building, which was destroyed by a fire in 741. A larger church was rebuilt in stone with room for 30 altars.

Multangular Tower

Ten-sided defensive tower that could have been over nine-metres tall, built by the Romans between 209 and 211 CE.

Homes and Shops

Items made by local craftspeople on sale here included wooden cups and bowls, jewellery, hats, clothes, shoes, brooches, buckles and combs.

Who Were the Vikings?

Vikings came from Norway, Sweden and Denmark. They were excellent sailors, fearsome warriors and clever traders. The Vikings' knowledge of the seas and tides allowed them to sail to coasts in Europe and beyond. They carried out many surprise raids on the English coast before eventually launching a bigger attack to invade areas deeper inland.

Cesspit

Toilet waste and other unwanted rubbish went into a cesspit – a simple hole in the ground – where it was left to rot and stink.

Coppergate

An important shopping street in the city. 'Coppergate' means 'street of the cup-makers'.

34

Cemetery

Many of the gravestones were decorated with images of legendary creatures such as dragons and giant snakes. Dogs were sometimes buried with their masters to keep them company on their way to the next life.

Saint Peter's School

Attached to York Minster. Founded by Saint Paulinus of York in 627, making it the fourth oldest school in the world. Strictly no admission if you were a girl!

King's Hall

Used for feasts that, in true Viking tradition, could often last for days. Decorated with fine tapestries on the walls and with long tables and benches for guests.

RIVER FOSS

Flows into the larger River Ouse. The city's location between two rivers made it much easier to defend.

Quayside

A bustling area of the city with ships arriving and traders buying and selling goods. The Viking trading network extended far and wide, including importing shells from the Indian Ocean and silks from China.

Fish Market

Fresh fish were sold here. Herrings were cheap and plentiful.

Blacksmiths

Blacksmiths were among the most important people in the city. They were skillful craftsmen who made tools such as needles, nails and knives as well as weapons for battle. They worked in tin and copper alloys as well as gold and silver.

Houses

The ever-expanding Jórvík included houses built in the traditional Viking way as well as in the Anglo-Saxon style, built at different points during its history.

Roman Walls

Defensive walls around the city built of limestone blocks, which were later reused by different conquering invaders.

Height of the Roman defensive walls:

About

2.5

metres

Number of times that Jórvík was invaded and changed hands:

At least

13

Population of Jórvík in 940:

Up to

10,000

Population of York today:

200,000

LIFE IN JÓRVÍK

With the Vikings in charge, Jórvík grew quickly in size and importance. The Vikings had an amazing trading network all over Europe, including places we know today as Russia, Iceland, Ireland and Turkey. Later on, they even sailed across the Atlantic Ocean to Greenland and North America. Jórvík became a thriving trading port where people spoke many different languages, while swapping and trading goods from all over the known world.

When the Boat Comes in

Vikings were extremely skilful sailors and brilliant navigators. Later in the Viking age, their secret weapon was their Viking 'longship', some of which were more than 20 metres in length. Longships were slender, fast and surprisingly strong. They could travel either by sail power or by manned oars, meaning that they didn't have to depend on the wind to get where they wanted to go. But the best thing about longships was the fact that they had shallow bottoms, so they could be sailed up small rivers and pulled up on beaches. This meant Vikings could launch sudden attacks against targets (like monasteries full of gold) on the coast without any warning.

Work and Play

There were no schools for Viking children. That might sound like good news, but in Jórvík, children were expected to work! They might help grown-ups in a family workshop. At home, they were expected to help with cooking and making clothes. It wasn't all work though. Viking kids had toys to play with, like carved wooden animals, board games, and musical instruments, such as pipes and drums.

Home Sweet Home

Traditional Viking homes had a long open fireplace, which was the centre of life for cooking and keeping warm. Despite having a hole in the roof, Viking houses were often full of smoke. Houses in Jórvík reflected the fact that the city was a real mixture of different cultures. Instead of having a grass turf roof as a Viking home would have, many were built from timber with an Anglo-Saxon thatched roof. The toilet was a hole, or cesspit, in the ground outside, and for toilet paper people used old pieces of cloth or a handful of moss.

Viking Feast

If there was something to celebrate, like a great victory or the return of an important warrior, then you can bet that the Vikings would throw a feast. These took place in the King's Hall and could go on for days. Vikings drank ale and mead from a hollow horn. While they ate, Vikings would be entertained by musicians and *skalds* (storytelling poets), who recited long poems about heroic acts, daring deeds and great battles.

Jórvík

UNITED KINGDOM

Tales of Asgard

People in Jórvík practised a mixture of religions. Some Vikings had converted to Christianity, while many others still worshipped the old Norse gods. Vikings believed in the gods of *Asgard*, a magnificent fortress in the sky reached by travelling along a rainbow bridge. The king of the gods was Odin, who had many children, including the mighty Thor, God of Thunder. Vikings believed that thunder and lightning were signs that Thor was riding through the sky.

BEIJING

1400s

Great Wall
1000 km North ↑

The Ming dynasty made the Great Wall much stronger than ever before, to keep out invaders at China's northern border.

In the 1400s, Beijing was the capital of China and one of the biggest cities in the world. China was ruled by the Ming dynasty, whose palace complex lay at the heart of their capital. This map shows the Imperial City, including the palace complex or 'Forbidden City', which no ordinary person was allowed to enter on pain of death.

Grand Canal

The canal transported grain, salt and other essential goods, and connected Beijing with the south of China.

City Walls

Bell Tower

Drums and bells announced the time of day.

Drum Tower

Gate of Western Peace

Forbidden City

The Imperial City

Great Ming Gate

This gate faced south, which was considered to be the most important direction.

Temple of Agriculture

The emperor came here to make offerings to the gods for a good harvest.

Temple of Heaven

THE IMPERIAL CITY

Gate of Earthly Peace

Jingshan Park
The soil used to form this hilltop park came from the digging of the moat.

Forbidden City
High walls and a wide moat surrounded the palace complex that's now known as the 'Forbidden City'.

Palace of Earthly Tranquility
The empress lived here.

Palace of Heavenly Purity
The emperor lived here.

Western Garden
The two gardens inside the Imperial City were only for the use of the emperor and government officials.

Hall of Supreme Harmony
This large building was used for special occasions with a magnificent golden throne on a high platform for the emperor.

Hall of Preserving Harmony

Hall of Central Harmony

TAIYE LAKE

Marble Imperial Carriageway
Made from a 250-tonne block of marble carved with clouds and dragons.

Gate of Eastern Peace

Imperial Ancestral Temple

Altar of Earth and Harvests

Gate of Accepting Heavenly Mandate

LIFE IN BEIJING

Beijing

When the Yongle emperor ruled China, he moved his capital city back to Beijing, as it had been decades earlier under the Mongol rulers. From this impressive newly built city, he ruled one of the biggest, oldest and wealthiest civilisations on Earth, which traded with countries as far away as Africa.

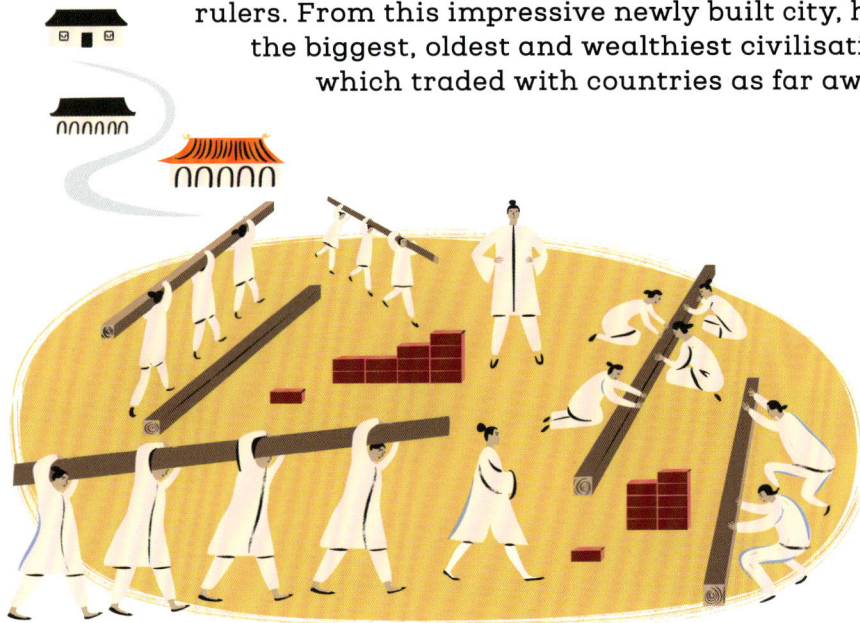

The Mighty Ming

The emperor needed a capital that would show the wealth and might of the Ming. So he built the Imperial City, and the Forbidden City within it, the biggest palace complex in the world. It took hundreds of thousands of craftspeople and labourers 14 years to complete. The walls around the palace complex hid it completely from the rest of Beijing.

Inside the Forbidden City

The southern part of the Forbidden City was for men only. Every day, male officials waited outside the Meridian Gate for the emperor's reception to begin at 5 a.m. There were strict rules about what they wore and where they stood, and all visitors to the emperor had to kneel and put their foreheads to the floor nine times to acknowledge his greatness.

Zheng He

★ FAMOUS FACE ★

The early Ming dynasty was a time of exploration, and the greatest explorer of all was Zheng He, who led expeditions by sea on behalf of the emperor. Together with hundreds of soldiers, he made seven voyages between 1405 and 1433, travelling to India, Japan, the Middle East and the East African coast. He brought back gifts including ostriches, zebras and giraffes, established valuable trade routes, and spread news to the wider world about the mighty Ming dynasty. Later Ming emperors ended these expensive voyages, but local trading by sea continued.

40

Imperial Family Life

The northern part of the Forbidden City was for the imperial family – and it was a very big family. As well as his principal wife, the Empress Xi, the emperor had many other wives, who also lived in the palace. Once these women had entered the Forbidden City, it was very rare for them to leave. Only the emperor could go wherever he wanted, whenever he wanted. All the emperor's children were known as 'children of the empress', whether their mother was the empress or one of the other wives, and there could be bitter competition among the sons to be named the next emperor. As in many other ruling families all over the world, only boys could grow up to rule China.

The End of an Era

The Ming dynasty lasted until 1644, when forces from the North came from beyond the Great Wall of China and seized Beijing, and the Qing dynasty began. Today, 600 years after the Forbidden City was built, and 100 years after China's last emperor, Beijing is still the capital city of China. Modern skyscrapers tower over temples, palaces and gardens many centuries old, and the Forbidden City is now a museum, open to everyone.

BEIJING IN NUMBERS

Size of Imperial City:

961
metres long
X
753
metres wide

Number of emperors who lived in the Forbidden City:

24
from the Ming and Qing dynasties

Population of Beijing in the 1400s:

Up to
500,000

Population of Beijing today:

21.7
million

GRANADA

Nestled at the bottom of the Sierra Nevada mountains in the country we now call Spain, the Islamic city kingdom of Granada was full of fruit trees, ornate gardens and shimmering fountains. Gleaming above the bustling streets and bazaars was the gorgeous Alhambra, home of the ruling sultan and his family.

Great Mosque

In the 1400s there were 137 mosques in the city of Granada. This one was the grandest.

Alcazaba

This mighty fortress guarded Granada and was also home to the sultans before the Alhambra was completed.

Great Bazaar

Silk was traded here, along with spices, vegetables and dried and fresh fruit, clothing, pottery, carpets, and enslaved people captured in battles with Christian armies.

Tea Shop

People met friends and made business deals in the city's many tea shops.

Alhóndiga

There were lots of these buildings in Granada in the 1400s. They served as roadside inns, markets and stores for the neighbourhood's grain and goods.

Hammam (Bathhouse)

People went to wash, socialise and relax in hammams.

42

Albaicín

The oldest part of the city, packed with houses and shops all crowded together in the narrow, winding streets.

Carmen

Villas with beautiful gardens in the Albaicín were (and still are) called 'carmenes'.

DARRO RIVER

Courtyard of the Lions

Generalife

This summer palace of the sultans was linked to the Alhambra by a covered walkway across the ravine that separated them.

Alhambra

This beautiful fortified palace complex included places for people to meet, palaces and spectacular gardens full of streams, pools and fountains.

43

Grand Designs

Colourful patterned tiles and ornate plasterwork decorated the Alhambra, while roses, orange trees and myrtle hedges filled the courtyards and gardens with scent and colour.

Empire

Granada was part of the Islamic Empire that stretched across southern Spain. Muslim people of North African and Arab heritage had conquered most of Spain several hundred years earlier. The word *granada* is Spanish for 'pomegranate'.

City Walls

Sierra Nevada Mountains

GRANADA IN NUMBERS

Number of mosques in Granada in the 1400s:

137

Number of mosques in Granada today:

2

Population of Granada in 1450:

50,000

Population of Granada today:

235,000

LIFE IN GRANADA

In the 700s, Muslim Berber and Arab invaders sailed from North Africa and went charging through Spain on horseback. They ruled over much of the country for hundreds of years. The citizens of the beautiful city kingdom of Granada were the last in Spain to live under Islamic rule, until the Islamic kingdom was finally overthrown.

SPAIN

Granada

Early Granada

People have lived in the area that's now Granada since the Stone Age. The ancient Romans came and went, leaving the aqueducts and sewers they'd built, and after them came the Visigoths (a Germanic people). Later on, the city's Jewish community named the town 'Garnata al-Yahud', which might be where the name Granada comes from.

Water Everywhere

Under Islamic rule, Granada grew from being a small settlement to a rich and beautiful city. The Berber and Arab settlers, who came from the deserts of North Africa, were experts in water engineering. They improved the ancient Roman aqueducts and sewers and channelled more fresh water to Granada for homes and for growing food. They also introduced new kinds of fruit and vegetables to Spain – oranges, lemons, apricots, bananas, spinach, celery and artichokes are just a few – as well as almonds, rice and sugar cane.

Baths and Gardens

The Muslim rulers built luxurious bathhouses, where they washed and also met for a chat and something to drink. The baths were covered in patterned tiles, with star-shaped multi-coloured glass skylights that lit the rooms in gorgeous colours. Granada's streets were lined with almond and orange trees, and houses often had lovely gardens. The most beautiful of all were in the Alhambra palace complex, where water flowed into pools and cascaded from fountains amongst the flower beds.

A Tale of Two Cities

Unlike Granada's clean, tree-lined streets, the streets of most European cities in the Middle Ages were foul-smelling and filthy, with the rivers used as a sewer. If they were sick, most Europeans had to hope for the best, while Granada's citizens were treated by skilled doctors.

45

★ FAMOUS FACE ★

Muhammed XII became the last sultan, or king, of Granada in 1482. He tried to expand his kingdom, but the rulers of the Christian kingdoms on either side had been united by marriage and had become too powerful. Muhammed was captured and imprisoned for three years. He was granted his freedom when he agreed to accept the rule of the invading Christian king and queen.

Muhammed XII

The End of an Era

King Ferdinand II of Aragon and Queen Isabella I of Castile married in 1469 and joined their kingdoms. Their army besieged the city of Granada for eight months before Muhammed XII surrendered, ending 700 years of Muslim rule in Spain in 1492. The new Christian rulers didn't keep their promise to let Muslim and Jewish people live alongside Christians in Granada. Many Islamic buildings were destroyed, and the Islamic Great Mosque was turned into a Christian cathedral.

VENICE

An extraordinary city where people use a network of canals to travel instead of roads, Venice was built on over a hundred small islands linked by bridges in a beautiful Italian lagoon. A city so powerful it was once its own city state (or country), the 'Republic of Venice' built a mighty sea empire and became the most important trading port of its time.

VENETIAN LAGOON

GRAND CANAL

Known to Venetians as the 'Canalazzo', this is the largest waterway through Venice.

Fondaco dei Turchi

This impressive palace was used by royals and other important people while they visited the city.

Rialto Quarter

This part of the city was full of traders selling spices and fine fabrics. Fresh fruit and vegetables arrived by barge daily.

Gondolas

The city's traditional mode of transport.

46

Merchant Ships

At any one time, there would have been dozens of ships loading and unloading goods from all around the world. These ranged from lace and glass made in Venice, to enslaved men, women and children from Europe to be sold in Northern Africa and the Middle East.

Murano

These seven small linked islands were famous for their glassmaking and made much of the glass for the whole of Europe.

Ca'd'Oro

The name of this great palace translates as the 'House of Gold'.

Rialto Bridge

The only bridge across the Grand Canal and the centre of the city.

Fondaco dei Tedeschi

Many Germans settled in Venice, and this is where they lived, worked and traded.

Santi Giovanni e Paolo

Known as the 'Pantheon of Venice', many of the city's *doges*, or rulers, are buried in this gothic church.

Saint Mark's Basilica

The most famous church in the city.

Doges' Palace

Saint Mark's Campanile

The first tower here was a lighthouse to help sailors navigate. A later version was used to imprison criminals before their execution.

Saint Mark's Square

The largest and most important public space in Venice. During Carnival, a six-week-long festival held at the end of December, Venetians would disguise themselves in masks and take to the squares to watch spectacles.

47

The Arsenal of Venice

The secret of the city's military success was the Arsenal, the largest shipbuilding facility in the world. It had a workforce of 16,000 people and, at full speed, it could build ten fully-armed ships in just six hours!

LIFE IN VENICE

Life in the city state of Venice was all about the sea, ships and selling things. With its incredible shipbuilders and access to trade routes from Europe and Africa to the Far East, Venice was one of the most powerful cities in the whole of Europe.

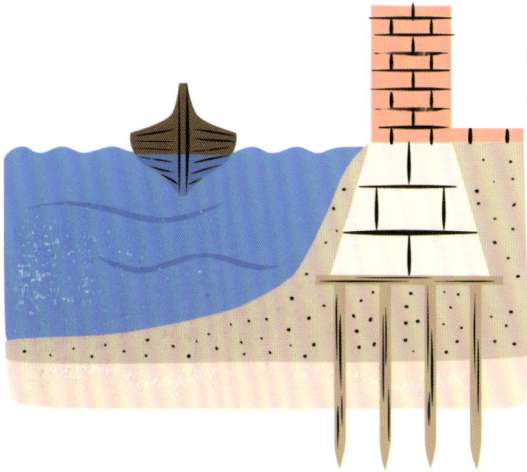

A Life on the Ocean Waves

Imagine building a city in the middle of the sea! The first settlers on Venice did just that, building on high-lying areas of a shallow lagoon. To stop their homes from sinking or flooding, they drove huge wooden poles deep into the sand and clay below the waterline, and then built a layer of marble on top to make strong, waterproof foundations.

Money, Money, Money

Venice was in the perfect position to trade with mainland Europe to the west and the Middle and Far East to the east. Wood, iron ore, wool, salt and even enslaved people were sent east and traded for spices, perfumes, amazing carpets, fine cloth, gold and silver and precious gems. The Venetians could then sell these exotic items on to the rest of Europe at a vast profit. However, with great success came great danger, as local pirates attacked the city's ships in an attempt to steal their share of the city's gold.

Marco Polo

★ FAMOUS FACE ★

Venice's most famous son was explorer and merchant Marco Polo. Polo joined his father's merchant trading business and spent a quarter of a century travelling as far as China. When he returned he wrote a book about his adventures. Over the years, the tales of Polo's travels have influenced many people including, centuries later, Christopher Columbus who was inspired to set sail across the Atlantic after reading it.

VENICE IN NUMBERS

Number of islands: **118**

Number of bridges: About **400**

Gondolas

The traditional way of travelling around Venice is in boats called gondolas. The boat is steered by a gondolier using a single oar to push the boat along. The boat's slim shape and flat underside are perfect for travelling through the narrow canals of the city.

Gondolier
This job often passed from father to son.

The Oar
Has a ribbed surface.

Passengers
Sit low near the waterline.

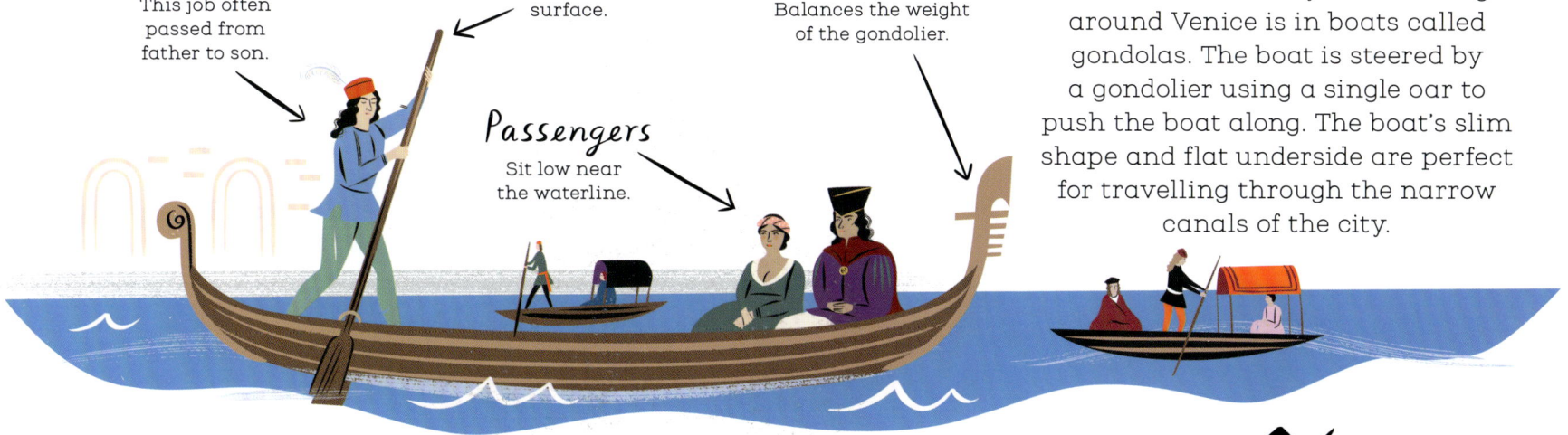

The Ferro
Balances the weight of the gondolier.

A Plague on All Your Houses

With maritime travellers arriving from all over the known world, accidentally importing diseases was a real problem. The plague had hit the population of Venice very badly several times. To help stop disease spreading, quarantine stations were set up where ships had to wait for 40 days before people were allowed on shore.

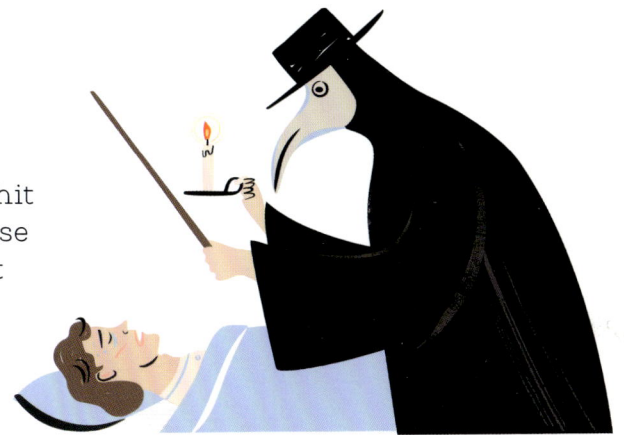

Living It Up

Rich Venetians were not shy about displaying their wealth. They loved festivals and carnivals, spending their money on the finest clothes and on making their homes look like royal palaces. They were so good at showing off that laws were passed to try and stop people wearing clothes of gold and silver material so the city appeared more modest. Not all people were rich, of course, and as ever the poor lived in terrible conditions.

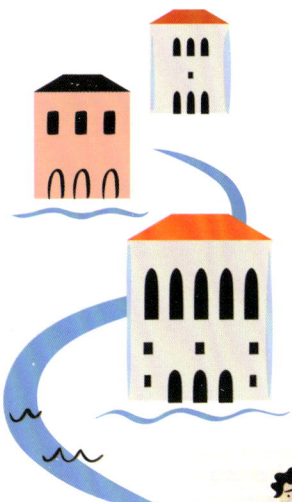

The End of an Era

Venice's trading empire lasted hundreds of years, but it eventually came to an end. Believing Venice was too powerful, many of its enemies and rivals formed an alliance called the 'League of Cambrai' and fought against Venice together. Around the same time, other cities and ports started trading directly with the spice merchants of the Far East and were able to cut the merchants of Venice out of their deals altogether.

Population in 1450: About 175,000

Population today: 55,000

BENIN CITY

In the middle of the West African rainforest, huge walls and deep moats surrounded a city that gleamed with brass. Benin City was the heart of a rich and powerful empire that stretched for hundreds of kilometres.

City Walls

The city was surrounded by enormous walls made from earth, and deep moats. At the time, these mighty walls were second in size only to the Great Wall of China. They enclosed 6,500 square kilometres of land and were built over hundreds of years.

Palm-oil Lamps

These massive metal lamps lit the streets close to the palace at night.

Streets

The city's streets were wide and straight and fanned out from the palace. They had an underground drainage system to carry away water in the rainy season.

Brass Casters

Working with brass was the city's most important trade.

IGUN STREET

City Plan

Different trades, or guilds, had their own special area of the city – carpenters, ivory carvers, weavers, potters, beadmakers, town criers, royal drummers and so on.

Atlantic Ocean
← 90 km Southwest

Ships sailed from Europe to the West African coast. The Europeans then travelled through the rainforest to trade with Benin City.

50

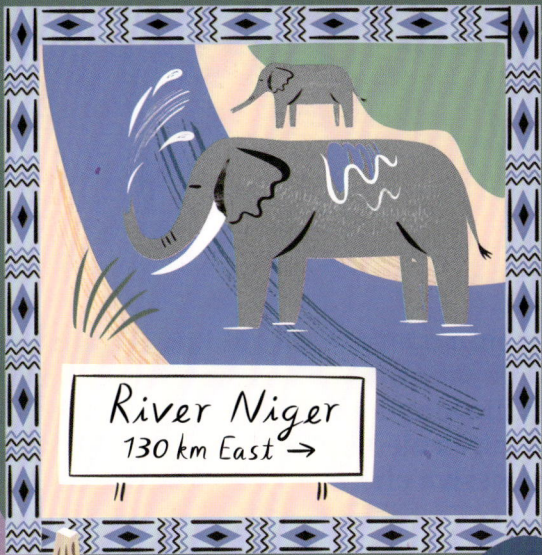

River Niger
130 km East →

Rainforest

The city was built in the rainforest, some of which was cleared for growing crops and farming.

Oba's Palace

The oba was the king of Benin. His palace was spectacular, with galleried courtyards and steep turrets, which were decorated with slithering snakes down the sides and birds with outstretched wings on top. The oba's family and royal attendants lived at the palace. His staff included acrobats, leopard hunters and handlers, and sorcerers!

Villages

Outside the city centre, people lived in villages, which were also surrounded by huge earth walls.

LIFE IN BENIN CITY

Over 1,000 years ago, people built a city in the middle of the rainforest in West Africa. By the 1400s, the forest city was rich and prosperous, with a beautiful palace for the oba who ruled the kingdom. A hundred years later, the kingdom had grown into a wealthy empire ruled by 'warrior kings', and Benin City was one of the most impressive city states in the medieval world.

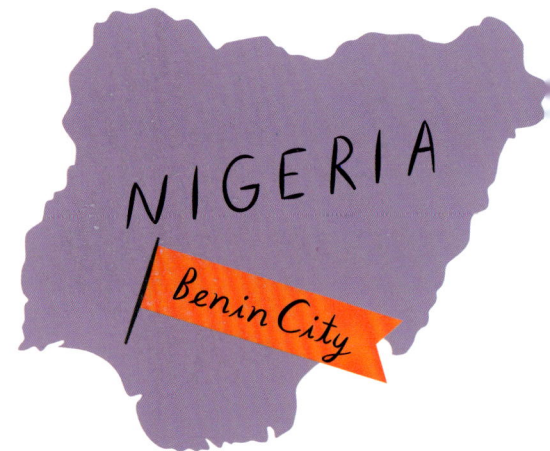

NIGERIA

Benin City

Making Money

The Kingdom of Benin became rich by trading its natural resources with other African countries, and, from the late fifteenth century, with Europe. When European traders first saw Benin City, they were amazed by its size, organisation and lack of crime: completely different from the overcrowded, dirty and dangerous cities in Europe. From Europe came cloth, guns, cowrie shells that the people of Benin used as money, and brass bracelets that were melted down to make objects for court and ritual use.

In return, Benin sold peppercorns, ivory from elephants' tusks, and leopard skins. There was also a trade in people, who were enslaved and sold to European slave traders. These people came from conquered lands, or from Benin itself. Enslaved people were shipped against their will to the Americas and Europe. Many of them died on the overcrowded slave ships, and those that survived were forced to work in appallingly harsh conditions.

Brass casters were the most important of all the guild workers in Benin. The sculptures they made were commissioned by the oba or made with his permission. Women were forbidden from touching the metal, or even from touching metal tools, and were only allowed to work in the weavers' guild, making textiles or spinning yarn.

The oba had hundreds of servants and courtiers living in his palace. As well as the sort of jobs you'd expect, like guarding, cooking and cleaning, some of the oba's staff had to walk the palace leopards, or perform magic!

A City Destroyed

By the 1800s, British merchants and government officials were trying to control trade with the Kingdom of Benin, because it produced lots of valuable palm oil and rubber. In 1897, a British naval expedition invaded Benin City and made it part of the British Empire. The city was destroyed, and many of its buildings were burned down. The city's beautiful brass plaques and other valuable objects were looted by the troops. The oba was exiled, and much of Benin's history, which had never been written down, was lost forever.

Benin Today

Sections of the original earth walls and moats can still be seen in Benin City, Nigeria, today. The oba's palace has been destroyed and rebuilt many times, but it's still there in the centre of the modern city. And Benin City is still famous for its brass: the street of the brass casters – Igun Street – is full of brass-casting workshops and beautiful metal sculptures for sale.

★ FAMOUS FACE ★

Oba Orhogbua was a warrior king who made the Benin Empire the largest it would ever be. Highly educated and with many wives and children, he was worshipped as a god, and hardly ever seen outside the palace. If he did leave the palace, people needed permission to look at him and had to approach him on their knees!

Oba Orhogbua

BENIN CITY IN NUMBERS

Length of earth walls around Benin City:

11
kilometres

Depth of moat around Benin City:

6
metres

Number of guilds in Benin City in the 1500s:

40

Population of Benin City today:

1.5
million

CUZCO

At its height, the Inca Empire ruled over five million people and was the largest ever seen in the Americas. At the very heart of the empire was its extraordinary capital of Cuzco. It was a fantastic mountain city of palaces and an amazing golden temple, laid out in the shape of a puma, one of the Inca's sacred animals.

Emperor's Palace

Home to the emperor or *Sapa Inca*. Each emperor built his own palace in the city, so the number gradually increased.

Throne of the Inca

Seats carved into natural rock. These were said to have been used by Inca nobles during important ceremonies.

Suntur Wasi

This circular weapons store was the tallest building in Cuzco.

Sacsayhuamán

This fortress is located 230 metres above the city. Its walls are constructed with huge stone boulders, some weighing 230 tonnes. It is said that the fortress forms the head and jaws of the city's puma shape.

Huacaypata

Cuzco was the centre of the Inca universe, and this large square, or plaza, was at the centre of Cuzco.

SAPHY RIVER

54

CUZCO

HANAN DISTRICT

HURIN DISTRICT

A Puma-shaped City

High up in the Andes Mountains is the puma-shaped city of Cuzco. The fortress temple of Sacsayhuamán makes up the puma's head, while two rivers outline the shape of its body.

Cusipata (Fortunate Terrace)

Covered with fine white sand that had been brought from the coast; gold, silver and precious shells were buried here during special religious ceremonies.

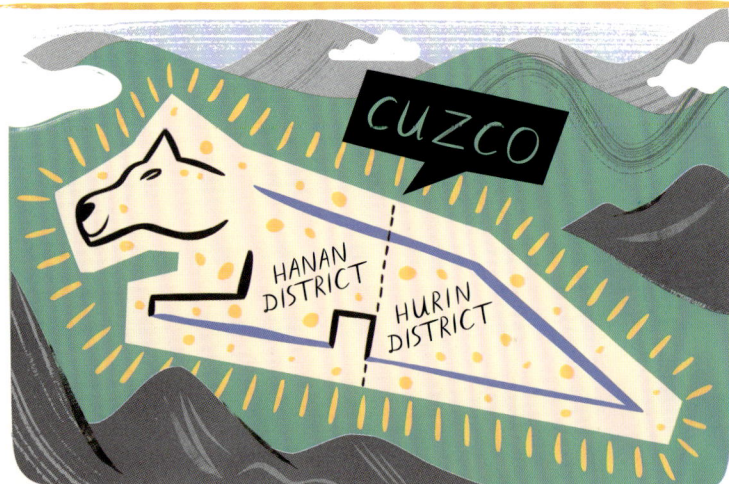

Andes Mountain Range

Cuzco is located at a height of 3,400 metres above sea level.

Tambomachay (Inca Baths)

Highways

The Inca built 40,000 kilometres of road through rainforests, deserts, mountains, valleys and grasslands to the four corners of the Inca Empire.

HANAN DISTRICT

HURIN DISTRICT

The city was divided into two districts. The upper part was the Hanan District and was the most prestigious part of the city. The lower part was the Hurin District.

TULLUMAYO RIVER

Coricancha (Temple of the Sun)

This glittering temple to the sun god, Inti, had its walls (inside and out) covered with over 700 sheets of gold. Sacrifices took place here.

Coricancha Complex (Golden Enclosure)

This group of important sacred buildings included the Temple of the Sun. It was also used as an astronomical observatory to study and predict the movements of stars and planets.

Three Rivers

Cuzco was built at the meeting point of three rivers, making it a sacred site to the Inca.

CHUNCHULLMAYO RIVER

LIFE IN
CUZCO

Until the start of the 1400s, Cuzco was little more than a small mountain town in the country now known as Peru. However, over the next 100 years, the city grew to become the capital of a vast empire stretching over 4,000 kilometres from north to south.

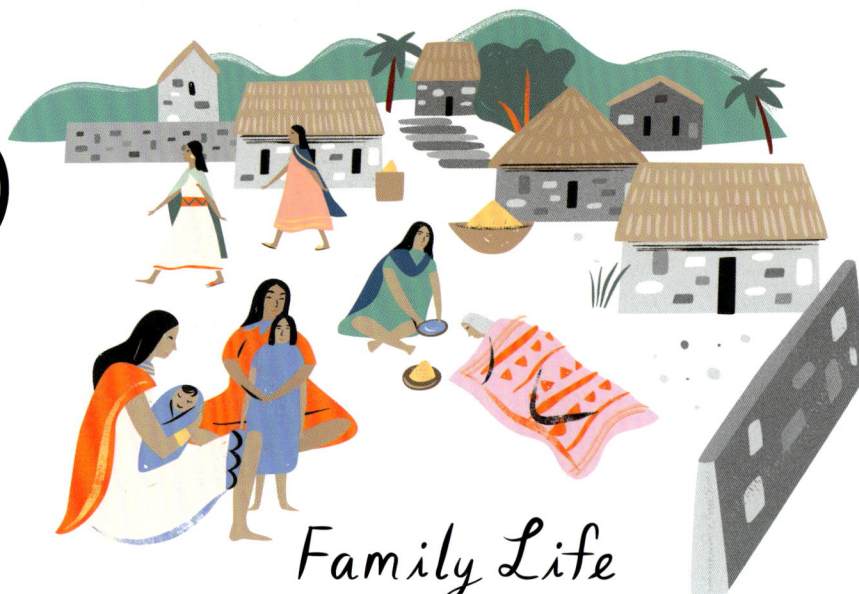

Family Life

Everyday life in Cuzco centred around small units called *ayllu*. An ayllu was a group of families who worked together and shared their homes and belongings like a large extended family. People were born into an ayllu and stayed in the same one all their lives. The Inca looked after their old and sick. If a person was injured or too frail to work, they would be given food and a home.

Reading by Weaving

Children from noble families went to school, although we don't know much about what they learned there, as the Inca never developed a system of writing. Instead, they used word of mouth to share information, and kept records by using colourful collections of knotted and twisted string called *quipu*. These were used for accounting and keeping a tally of crops and people – but may also have been used as maps or to store other information.

If they weren't from a noble family, then children had to start work when they were very young. They were taught skills such as weaving, growing corn and potatoes or caring for alpacas and llamas.

Cashless Society

The Inca did not use money or pay taxes. People usually contributed to society by spending a certain number of days every year working for the empire, from building roads to caring for the emperor and his family.

Building Blocks

The Inca were highly skilled in stonework and engineering. They built walls by cutting huge blocks into irregular shapes and fitting them together perfectly so that there were no gaps. They also built aqueducts to channel water away from buildings and roads into the fields and even invented suspension bridges to cross rivers and valleys.

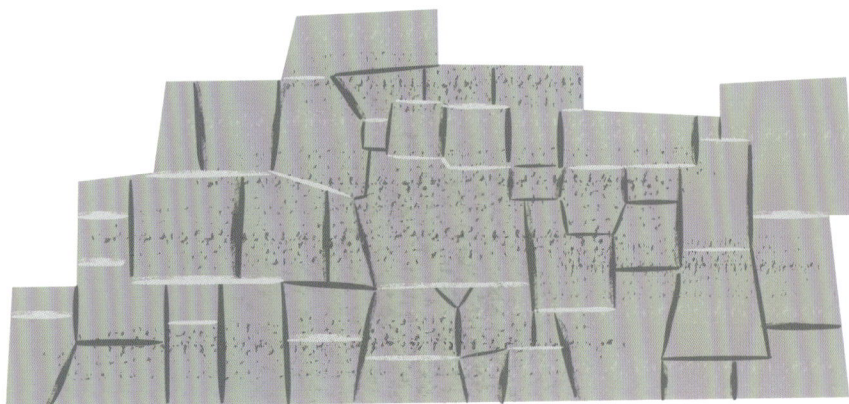

Gods and Sacrifice

The Inca worshipped many different gods. Their religious practices included saying prayers, fasting and sacrificing both animals and sometimes humans, including children. Many sacrifices might be offered on one day. Human sacrifice was used to ward off things such as military defeats, famine and plagues. Animals and foods were used for daily rituals such as throwing corn onto a fire to welcome the return of the sun each morning.

Going for Gold

The Inca believed that gold was the sweat of the sun god, Inti, and were incredibly skilled at making fine gold jewellery, statues and decorations.

Ask Your Mummy

When an emperor died, his body was mummified and kept at his palace. The mummies of old rulers were often brought to religious ceremonies dressed in their finest clothes so that offerings of food and drink could be made to them. The Inca believed that, after death, an emperor's spirit stayed in his body. The current emperor would also visit the mummified remains of his ancestors to ask their advice on important problems.

PERU

Cuzco

The End of an Era

The mighty Inca Empire began to crumble in the 1530s when Spanish invaders began a violent and bloody campaign of conquest, overthrowing the emperor. Further weakened by a civil war between the former emperor's sons, around 90 per cent of the surviving Inca population died from smallpox and other deadly diseases brought by the war-waging Europeans.

CUZCO IN NUMBERS

Height above sea level:

3,400
metres

Length of the Inca road system:

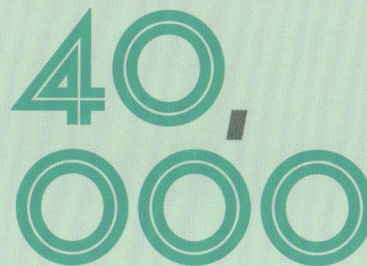

40,000
kilometres

Population of Cuzco in 1510:

Up to

200,000

Population of Cuzco today:

400,000

TENOCHTITLÁN

Around 1520

The Aztecs were fierce warriors who forged an empire that stretched across what's now Mexico. They built their capital on a marshy island in the middle of a lake — an astonishing city of pyramid temples, enormous palaces and networks of canals.

LAKE TEXCOCO

Legend says that the Aztecs had been told to build their city where they saw an eagle perched on a cactus.

← TEPEYACAC →

Canals

The Aztecs used canals for transporting people and goods.

← TLACOPÁN

Causeways →

Three long causeways linked Tenochtitlán to the shore, including drawbridges that could be pulled up, making the city into a fortress.

Sacred Precinct

IXTAPALAPA →

Valley of Mexico

This large valley is 2,200 metres above sea level.

Floating Islands

Crops grew on these man-made islands, as well as within the main city. As there were no large animals to provide poo to fertilise crops, human poo was collected and used instead.

SACRED PRECINCT

This was the centre of religious life, and where many of the most important religious ceremonies, including human sacrifice, took place.

Great Temple

Many thousands of men, women and children were sacrificed to the Aztec gods here, which was seen as a great honour.

Emperor's Palace

Built especially for Aztec leader Montezuma II, this enormous palace had 300 rooms, beautiful gardens and even a zoo!

Temalacatl

A gladiator stone, where captured warriors were made to fight.

← TEPEYACAC

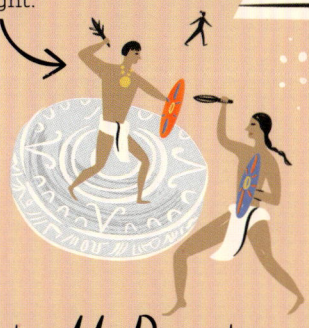

IXTAPALAPA →

59

Skull Racks

The skulls of sacrifice victims were displayed here. Some racks were said to hold up to 60,000 skulls.

Great Market

Tens of thousands of people flocked here every day to buy and sell everything from sweet potatoes to parrots.

Ball Court

The national game was *ullamaliztli*, a ball game that was extremely important to the ancient Aztecs. Symbolic games were sometimes played here – with a whole team being sacrificed after the match.

TLACOPÁN

Temple of Quetzalcóatl

LIFE IN TENOCHTITLÁN

The beautiful island capital of the Aztecs, Tenochtitlán, now lies beneath today's Mexican capital, Mexico City. Yet 500 years ago, before Europeans set foot in Tenochtitlán, city life had many similarities as well as some huge differences.

Aztec City Life

By 1519, perhaps as many as 300,000 people lived in Tenochtitlán. The closer to the city centre a person or family lived, the more important they were. Grand two-storey houses were for nobles and important warriors, while ordinary people lived in one-storey houses – any more than one floor and the punishment was death!

Keeping Clean

Unlike European cities at the time, where people emptied chamber pots into the streets, thousands of enslaved people and servants were employed to keep Tenochtitlán clean. Fresh water was carried into the city by two aqueducts, public steam rooms and toilets were built in every neighbourhood, and poo was carried by canoe to the fields to be used as fertiliser.

School for All

There were separate schools for boys and girls, and also for ordinary and noble children. Girls' education concentrated on looking after the home, while a young Aztec boy might grow up to become a farmer, a trader or a warrior. All children were also taught about religion, and some grew up to become priests and priestesses.

TENOCHTITLÁN IN NUMBERS

Size of Tenochtitlán: **13** square kilometres

Size of modern Mexico City: **1,485** square kilometres

Religious Sacrifices

At the top of the Great Temple, hundreds of human sacrifices took place every year. Some of the ceremonies could be gruesome. Strange though it may seem to us, being chosen to feed the gods with your heart and blood was seen as a great honour. Victims were often the strongest and most handsome prisoners of war, but sometimes they could be enslaved people, *ullamaliztli* (ball game) players, or ordinary adults and children.

WHAT'S IN A NAME?

The Aztecs had some poetic names such as Cozamalotl for a girl, which means 'rainbow', and Huitzilin for a boy, meaning 'hummingbird'. Both boys and girls could be called Eztli, which means 'blood'!

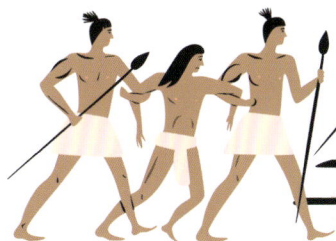

Montezuma II

★ FAMOUS FACE ★

Montezuma II was the Aztec emperor when the Spanish arrived at Tenochtitlán in 1520. He made the invaders welcome – possibly because he was setting a trap for their leader, Hernán Cortés. Montezuma died while he was in Spanish custody, and the Aztecs blamed the Spanish for their emperor's death. Cortés and his army were almost destroyed when they tried to leave the city.

MEXICO

Tenochtitlán

The End of the Aztecs

Within a few years, the Spanish had killed all of Montezuma's successors and as good as enslaved the Aztec people. They destroyed Tenochtitlán, building their own city on its ruins. Many Aztecs died of the diseases the Europeans brought with them, but many lived on and became part of the new Mexico.

Population of Tenochtitlán around the 1520s:
Up to 300,000

Population of modern Mexico City: 8.9 million

DELHI

RIVER

Delhi and its surrounding area in India has been inhabited for more than 3,000 years. Many different cities were built in the same area over the centuries. When each city was captured or destroyed, a new city was built nearby. The Mughal capital of Shahjahanabad (today known as Old Delhi) was created around 1638-48 when Shah Jahān, the fifth Mughal emperor, decided to move the royal court from Agra. A huge building programme began. Just 10 years later, the city stood ready to be occupied, with the impressive Red Fort standing guard over the streets of houses and shops.

FURTHER SOUTH

Delhi

Agrasen ki Baoli
Impressive stepwell dating back to the thirteenth century.

Humayun's Tomb and Nizamuddin Dargah
Humayun's Tomb was built in 1565 for the second Mughal emperor. Nizamuddin Dargah is one of the holiest places in Delhi.

Qutb Minar and Iron Pillar
Five-storey tower built in 1193 to mark a victory of the Muslim sultans. It is 73 metres high, making it the tallest free-standing brick minaret in the world. Near the Qutb Minar is an amazingly ancient iron pillar that dates back to the fourth century.

Begum ka Bagh
Local parkland which was surrounded by streets of bazaars.

Bazaars
The area around Chandni Chowk was full of crowded, narrow streets packed with shops selling everything from spices, textiles, carpets and jewellery, to leather shawls, quilts and paper. Customers would barter for the best price they could get.

Kalan Masjid
Built in 1387. Some people call it the 'Black Mosque.'

Ajmeri Gate
One of the 14 entrance gates in the city wall.

THE RED FORT

This stunning palace-fort was built to be the base of Mughal power by Shah Jahān.
It took nine years to build and was named for its battlements made from red sandstone.
It includes six gateways, royal apartments, bathhouses, towers and pavilions.
Many of its rooms were decorated with gold, silver and precious stones.

YAMUNA

This 1,375-kilometre-long river flows past the Red Fort.

Shahi Burj

One of Shah Jahān's favourite places to work.

Chhatta Chowk

A covered bazaar next to the Red Fort specialising in luxury goods such as silk and jewels.

Diwan-i-Aam

A huge hall supported by 60 stone pillars where the emperor held daily audiences with his subjects.

Lahori Gate

The main entrance to the Red Fort, built from red sandstone.

Chandni Chowk

Built as a grand ceremonial road for processions from the Red Fort (via the Lahori Gate) to the huge mosque of Jama Masjid.

Jama Masjid

The largest mosque in India, which took 5,000 workers six years to build. Known locally as the 'Friday Mosque', up to 20,000 people can pray here at once.

City Walls

Originally made of mud, and later replaced by red stone, this ran around the outskirts of the city.

Turkman Gate

Number of gates in Delhi's
original city walls:

14

Number of gates that
survive in Delhi today:

3

Population of Delhi in 1660:

50,000

Population of Delhi today:

11

million

LIFE IN DELHI

Delhi

INDIA

Delhi's central northern location meant that it was in the path of anyone invading from the north. Having captured and ransacked the city, invading forces would often decide to stay here or to build their own 'superior' city because its position was so desirable. This has meant that Delhi is one of the oldest continually inhabited areas in the world and one of the longest serving capital cities.

Empire Builders

Between 1527 and 1707, six great Mughal emperors ruled over India. These Mughal rulers had great military skills, but also established a stable, inclusive government by including people of different religions, such as Hindus. This age of Islamic rule was a golden age for art, literature and science. The Mughal emperors had a special passion for constructing amazing buildings.

Wildlife

Delhi was surrounded by thick forests of Indian pine trees that were home to many kinds of wildlife. Indian elephants are smaller than their African cousins and are intelligent animals that are easy to train. They were used for transport and to move large objects for building projects.

Beauty and Grace

The Taj Mahal in the city of Agra is one of the most famous buildings in the world and was also built by Shah Jahān, the man who founded Delhi. The Taj Mahal was built as a garden-tomb, to try and create an earthly image of the Islamic garden of paradise. Its white marble building blocks were carried over 300 kilometres by 1,000 elephants. (Not all at once!)

Altogether, it took 20,000 workers over 17 years to build it. The Mughal builders believed that flowers were symbols of heaven, so detailed and intricate flower designs appear all over the Taj Mahal in floors, walls and ceilings. This amazing building has been described as 'a prayer, a vision, a dream, a poem, a wonder'. It is often regarded as a powerful symbol of love because it was built by Shah Jahān for his wife.

WHAT'S IN A NAME?

Legend says that the city of Delhi was named after a king called Raja Dhilu, who ruled the area in the first century BCE. The city has been known by many names over the years, including Dehli, Dilli, and Dhilli.

Inspiring Art

The Mughal rulers of Delhi, and their queens, were great supporters of the arts. In particular, they admired a style called 'miniature painting' involving the creation of very detailed pictures, often of animals or plants. Usually, these were small works used in books or diaries. The Mughal emperors encouraged Persian painters of miniatures to move to India. Here, their miniature style fused with more local traditions to create a burst of creativity and energy in Mughal art.

Family Life

For normal people, life in Delhi revolved around being part of a family. The extended family would all share a house, including aunts, uncles, grandparents, cousins and often more distant relatives. Traditions and religious festivals and dates were very important in both family life and the wider community.

AMSTERDAM

1670s

In the seventeenth century, the city of Amsterdam became the most successful trading and financial centre in Europe. Ships from Holland carried more cargo around the globe than those from all other European countries combined, with merchants trading in spices and other rare goods and making huge profits. The city's canal system transported the goods to buyers around Amsterdam and beyond.

Singel Canal

Has encircled the city since the Middle Ages, acting as a defensive moat.

BROUWERSGRACHT CANAL

Built as a town hall for the city, using yellow sandstone.

Keizersgracht Canal

The widest of the major canals in the city, dug in 1615.

KEIZERSGRACHT CANAL

Royal Palace of Amsterdam

LIJN BAANSGRACHT CANAL

Rope Walks

Rope was essential to a bustling port city, and making it required long, narrow production areas for twisting the strands.

PRINSENGRACHT CANAL

Named after the Prince of Orange and built in 1612. This is the longest of the main canals.

HERENGRACHT CANAL

Also known as the Patricians' Canal or Lords' Canal. Includes the 'Golden Bend' with its impressive mansions.

Dam Square

The main city square and site of the first dam across the Amstel river.

City Walls

Built to protect the city against invasion.

Stocks and Shares

In 1602, Amsterdam became home to the world's first stock exchange, where investments were made and shares were traded. This made the rich people in the city very, very rich. Their success paid for the growth of Amsterdam and its network of beautiful canals. This period was known as the Dutch 'Golden Age'.

66

The Herring Packers' Tower

Part of the medieval city defences.

SINGEL CANAL

IJ BAY

PORT OF AMSTERDAM

Used as early as the thirteenth century, and one of the busiest ports in Europe.

67

Oude Kerk

The oldest parish church in the city, dating back to 1213.

Amsterdam Stock Exchange

The oldest stock exchange in the world founded in 1602.

Lastage

Marshy land to the east of the city. Now a port and industrial area.

The Munttoren Tower

One of the main gates in the medieval city wall. *Munt* means 'mint' and this tower was used to mint, or make, coins in the seventeenth century.

Hortus Botanicus

This botanical garden was created in 1638 as a herb garden for doctors and physicians. It is the oldest botanical garden in Europe.

Jewish Quarter

Jewish people came to settle in the city because of its religious freedom.

AMSTEL RIVER

Flows through the city and gave Amsterdam its name.

Number of bridges:

1,700

Number of islands:

90

Population of
Amsterdam in 1670s:

193,000

Population of
Amsterdam today:

860,000

LIFE IN AMSTERDAM

So exactly how did the little city of Amsterdam in the Netherlands come to conquer the world? There were three main factors. Firstly, the city's stock exchange was a new idea and meant that merchants could spread their investments so they wouldn't lose all their money if one ship sank. Secondly, the people of Amsterdam were said to be extremely hardworking and many were well educated. And lastly, the country had a history of seafaring, with skilled and experienced sailors.

Water, Water Everywhere

Amsterdam is built on swampland and is really a collection of islands. It's most famous for the impressive 100-kilometre network of canals that earned Amsterdam the nickname of 'Venice of the North'. The very first canal acted as a defensive moat around the city. During its so-called Golden Age, more canals were built, with plots for large, expensive homes sold along the sides. In 1613, the city authorities started an even more ambitious programme of canal building, creating canals that were two to three metres deep. New parts of the city were carefully planned so that roads, canals and bridges all linked up.

★ FAMOUS FACE ★

The Golden Age of Amsterdam was also a golden age for its art world. Artists found themselves in the happy position of sharing the city with a large number of rich merchants with money to spend. One of the stars of the art world was Rembrandt van Rijn, who moved to Amsterdam when he was a young man. He and his students churned out portraits for anyone who could pay them, especially wealthy merchants. Rembrandt was well known for his grumpy manner, but his audience loved his work and his art studio became one of the largest in Holland. He is recognised as one of the greatest painters who ever lived.

Rembrandt van Rijn

Two's Company

Not only was Amsterdam home to the world's first published newspaper during the Golden Age, but it saw the birth of the world's first multinational company as well. Up until then, only rich governments could afford to run companies outside their home country. When the Amsterdam Stock Exchange started, a number of smaller trading companies joined together to form the Dutch East India Company, which was granted sole rights to the Dutch spice trade for 21 years. Being the only company allowed to import high-profit spices meant that it soon became as powerful as a small country, with its own fleet of ships and its own navy.

Flower Power

The Dutch certainly loved their flowers, especially tulips. During Amsterdam's Golden Age, people went crazy for tulips, with bulbs being sold for extraordinary prices. People bought the bulbs as an investment, hoping to sell them on for a large profit. The more exotic the colours, the higher the price. At one point, a single bulb of an unusually colourful tulip was valued at ten times a carpenter's annual salary! Prices were too silly to stay that high for long. When tulip mania wilted, they dropped suddenly and many people were left badly out of pocket.

Amsterdam

NETHERLANDS

The End of an Era

After 100 years of success, Holland became weakened by continuing its expensive and damaging wars with other countries, such as France and England. Gradually, all along the world's trading routes, the ships from Amsterdam's port were overtaken by newer, faster vessels from rival countries.

PARIS

Towards the end of the eighteenth century, Paris was a city of 'haves' and 'have-nots'. King Louis XVI and his wife, Marie-Antoinette, lived in luxury and ruled France with absolute power, while many ordinary people were shockingly poor. Eventually the anger of the French people boiled over, leading to a violent revolution. The king and queen were publicly executed, and France became a republic for the first time.

Jardin des Tuileries

Musée du Louvre

Home to one of the most important art collections in the world.

Place de la Révolution

The public square where King Louis XVI, and later his wife, Queen Marie-Antoinette, were executed.

Dôme des Invalides

Commissioned by the 'Sun King', Louis XIV, this extravagant church was used by the royal family for prayers and Mass.

Île de la Cité

This little island was the first part of Paris inhabited in around 250 BCE. The first settlers were known as the *Parisii*, from which Paris gets its name.

Hôtel National des Invalides

A hospital and long-term home for France's injured soldiers. Constant wars meant it was a busy place.

Versailles
↙ 20 km Southwest

The king's palace, Versailles, was the largest in Europe. The grandeur of its buildings and gardens was legendary.

City Walls

Built in 1784 by Louis XVI, partly to defend Paris and partly to enable taxes to be collected on goods entering the city.

Sainte-Chapelle

This church is known as the 'miracle of light' because of its amazing stained-glass windows.

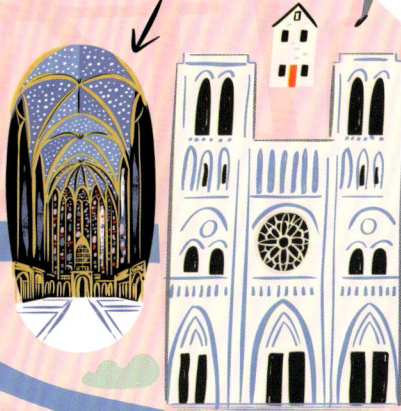

Place Royale

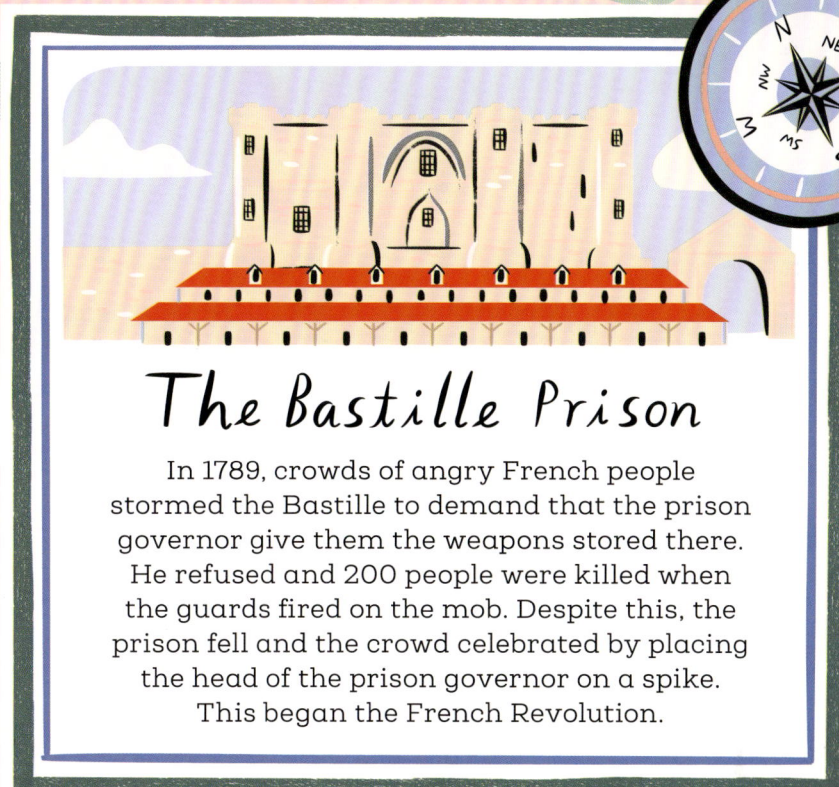

The Bastille Prison

In 1789, crowds of angry French people stormed the Bastille to demand that the prison governor give them the weapons stored there. He refused and 200 people were killed when the guards fired on the mob. Despite this, the prison fell and the crowd celebrated by placing the head of the prison governor on a spike. This began the French Revolution.

Notre-Dame Cathedral

One of the city's oldest and most impressive buildings, it took 200 years to complete.

Faubourg Saint-Antoine

Warren of narrow passageways and streets containing markets, butchers, carpenters, printers and other trades.

Le Boucher

Panthéon

Jardin du Luxembourg

The most beautiful gardens in the city, containing fountains, sculptures and perfect lawns.

Bibliothèque Nationale de France

The national library contained a copy of every French book printed since 1537.

Le Monde

Faubourg Saint-Marcel

Location of a foul-smelling tannery (leather-making factory) and many of the city's poorest people.

Catacombs

Old mines under the city were filled with millions of bones from the packed city graveyards.

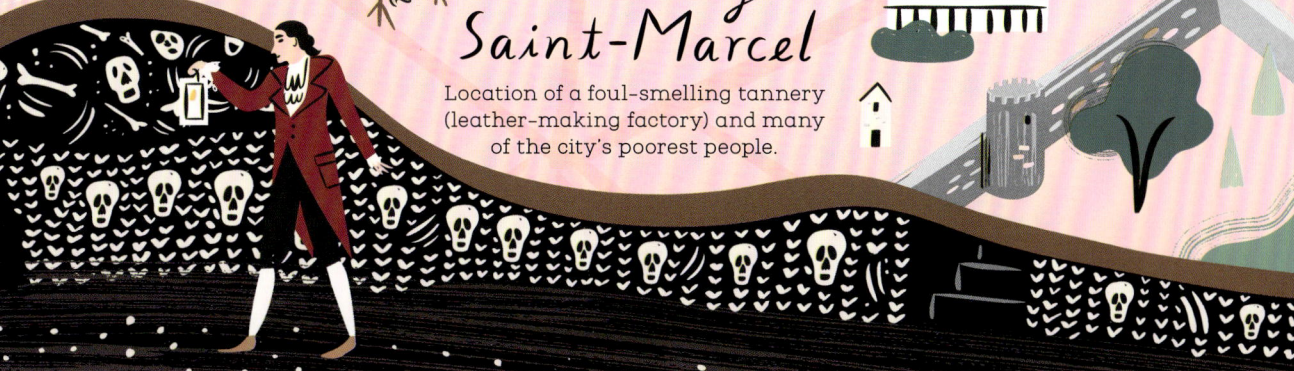

RIVER SEINE

LIFE IN PARIS

Several years of crop failures along with very harsh winters left many in 1780s Paris nearly starving to death. To be poor in Paris at this time meant to have nothing – no job, no warm clothes, no shelter and often not even a crust of bread to eat.

Rich and Poor

The rich had as much food as they could eat brought to them by maids in their huge, fancy houses. For the poor it was a different story – they often had nothing to eat at all, or even a place to call home. Rich children had private tutors, while most poor children could not read or write. Wealthy children played with toys such as wooden animals and china dolls, and sometimes even gruesome toy guillotines (miniature versions of the kind used to behead the king and queen!), while poor children had to make do with roughly carved wooden dolls.

Health Warning!

Diseases were common in the crowded and dirty city. Children born to poor parents had only a 50 per cent chance of surviving the first year of life! Even in rich households, poor hygiene and lack of medical knowledge meant that many children did not make it to adulthood.

The Reign of Terror

Getting rid of the monarchy proved to be a lot easier than setting up a new, fairer system of government. Paris turned into a dangerous, violent place for the best part of two decades, with the newly formed Committee of Public Safety taking over the revolutionary government and arresting up to 300,000 people on suspicion of being 'against' the revolution. At least 17,000 of this number were executed, some of them children as young as ten, with 10,000 more people dying in prison, sometimes without a trial.

★ FAMOUS FACE ★

Marie-Antoinette was the last queen of France. Born in Austria and married to the future king of France at just 14 years of age, she was unpopular with the public as the French were often at war with her home country. During the 1780s, she became more unpopular still due to her lavish spending on clothes and wigs at a time when many people in the country could barely afford to eat. When told the people were angry because of the lack of bread, she is supposed to have said: "Let them eat cake."

Marie-Antoinette

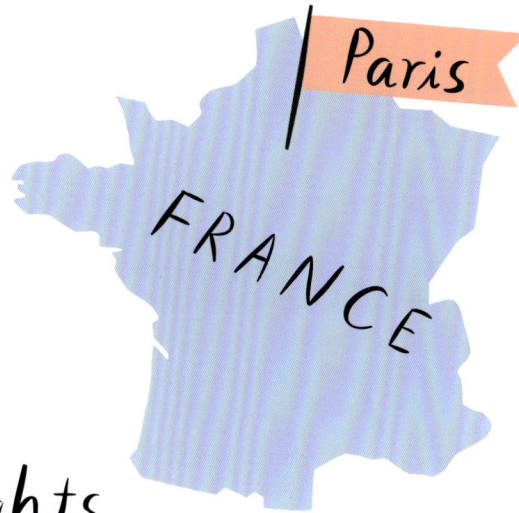

Human Rights

A Declaration of the Rights of Man

Paris

FRANCE

As a direct result of the French Revolution, a document was produced called *A Declaration of the Rights of Man and of the Citizen*. This was the first declaration in the world to set out ideas about human dignity, rights and equality.

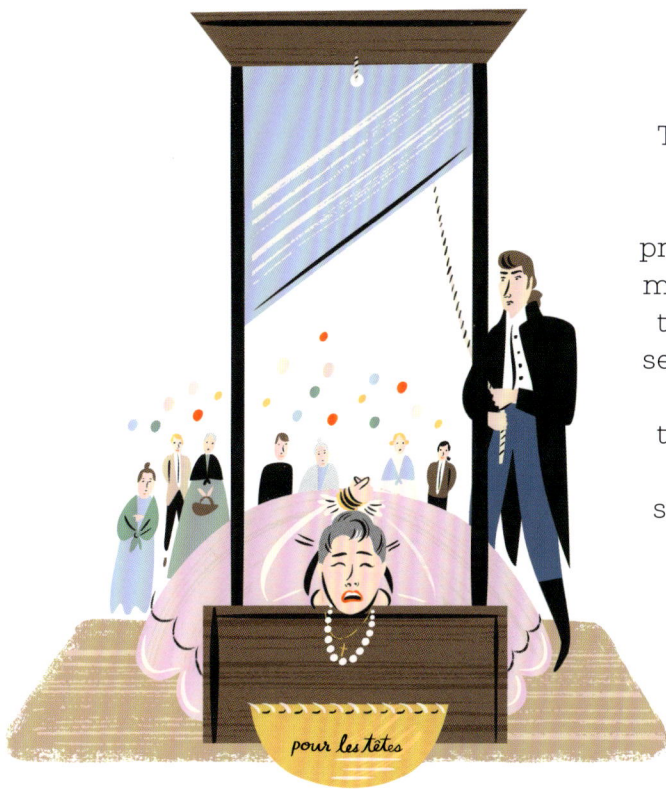

Chop, Chop

The guillotine was a fearsome death machine that dropped a blade upon the neck of a prisoner to cut off their head. All men and women, from common thieves to the monarchy, were sentenced to death by guillotine during the revolution. Using the same method of execution for rich and poor alike was supposed to symbolise that all people were equal.

pour les têtes

New Order

Despite its brutal tactics, the revolutionary government failed to establish itself securely and, a few years later, power was seized by the most successful officer in the French army, Napoleon Bonaparte. Within a few years, Napoleon had crowned himself emperor and France was once again under the absolute rule of one person.

PARIS IN NUMBERS

Number of people executed during the French Revolution:

17,000

Size of Paris today:

105 square kilometres

Population of Paris in 1789:

600,000

Population of Paris today:

2.25 million

SYDNEY

For tens of thousands of years, the Eora people lived on the shores of a beautiful natural harbour in Australia. Their lives changed forever when people arrived from the other side of the world to start a prison colony in 1788. Within 100 years, the colony had become Australia's first city – Sydney.

Sydney Harbour and the Eora

There were thousands of people living around the harbour when the British ships arrived in 1788. Those original inhabitants were part of the Eora Nation, which had 29 different clans, such as the Gadigal people, who lived on the south side of the harbour. Many of their descendants still live there today.

Military Hospital

Saint Philip's Church

Rock Art

In the sandstone rock around Sydney are hundreds of pictures of fish, whales, animals and people. These were made by members of the Eora Nation for thousands of years to record their stories and beliefs, and to document the new arrivals.

DARLING HARBOUR

Darling Harbour

Ships packed with goods for trade came to Sydney from China, India, America and Britain.

← 26 km West

Male Orphan School

Despite the name, not all of the children sent to orphan schools were orphans. Here, boys were taught basic maths, reading and writing, and left when they were about 15 to become farm labourers or apprentices to tradesmen.

Many of Sydney's roads were built on the walking tracks of the Eora people.

Ancient Roads

74

SYDNEY HARBOUR

Sydney Cove

The first ships to bring British convicts to Australia dropped anchor here. It was a gathering place for the Eora people, who called it 'Warrang'. The Eora people were banned from visiting the site by the government in the late 1800s.

Bennelong Point

The first British governor, Arthur Phillip, had a house built here for Bennelong, an Aboriginal man who was first captured by the colonists but became a friend of the governor. Today it's the site of the Sydney Opera House.

Tank Stream

After the British arrived, the main water source for the Gadigal people became too polluted to drink from any longer.

Government House

The governor's house and one of the oldest buildings in Sydney.

Farm Cove

The Eora people called this area 'Wuganmagulya', where clans came together for ceremonies. Despite its importance, the British took it over and tried to grow crops, without much success.

Government Stables

Government Domain

Part of the grounds of the governor's house.

Female School of Industry

Girls were taught basic maths, reading and writing and trained to be domestic servants.

Woolloomooloo Bay

Saint James' Church

Convict Hospital

Hyde Park

Sydney's central park was named after a famous park in London, England.

Convicts' Housing

When the settlement was first built, the convicts lived in simple huts or tents. They were put to work building roads, houses and public buildings in the new settlement.

Windmills

The first windmill was built on Flagstaff Hill to make flour for the colony. Windmills were the tallest buildings in Sydney at the time.

Australian Museum

Australia's oldest museum.

Soldiers' Barracks

LIFE IN SYDNEY

The first peoples of the Sydney area lived in small groups, and ate food they caught in the sea, or hunted or gathered on land. In the late 1700s, their way of life began to change dramatically, and by the 1830s, Sydney had become a city. But the Eora people survived, and are still there today.

AUSTRALIA

Sydney

An Englishman Down Under

In 1770, Captain James Cook became the first European to set foot on the east coast of Australia at Botany Bay, near Sydney. He planted a flag at Possession Island in the north and claimed eastern Australia for Britain, despite the fact there were people who already lived there, then sailed off to explore other parts of the world.

Punishments and Prison Ships

The city of Sydney started as a colony for prisoners. In Britain at the time, people could be hanged just for stealing a loaf of bread, as well as for terrible crimes like murder. But some criminals were shipped to a far-off colony instead of being put to death.

In 1787, 11 ships set sail from England to Australia carrying 775 prisoners: men, women and children as young as nine years old. Most of them had been convicted of theft, and many had stolen food because they were hungry. At first, conditions for prisoners in the colony were terrible – there wasn't enough food, there were outbreaks of disease and punishments were brutal.

SYDNEY IN NUMBERS

About 5 million
Population of Sydney today:

Number of prisoners transported from England to Australia:
About 160,000

The Eora and the New Arrivals

The British settlers brought new diseases that killed hundreds of Eora – as many as 80 per cent within the first few years. The settlers also took over the Eora people's land, hunting grounds and waterways, and most of them had little respect for Eora culture.

Some Eora saw cooperating with the settlers as the best way to survive, while others decided to fight, and many of the Eora people were killed. Afterwards, the survivors found new ways to live on their traditional land as the city grew across it. On 26 January 1938, 150 years after the first convict ships had arrived, Aboriginal people in Sydney and their supporters organised a Day of Mourning to protest about their treatment. It was an important step towards equal rights for the original peoples of Australia.

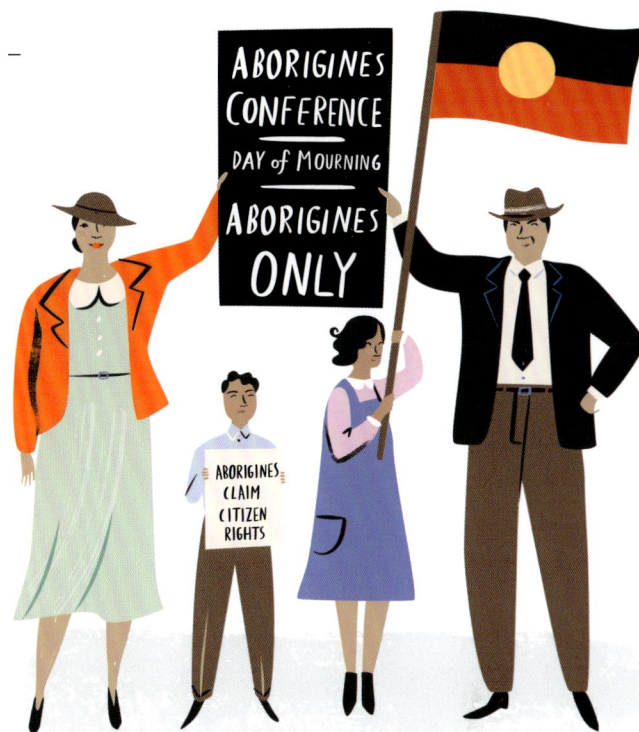

ABORIGINES CONFERENCE DAY of MOURNING ABORIGINES ONLY

ABORIGINES CLAIM CITIZEN RIGHTS

Sydney Life

By the 1830s, convicts were still being sent to Sydney, but their gruelling three-month journey ended at a flourishing new city. By this time, freed convicts lived in the city alongside new arrivals from Britain and Ireland, who had come to Sydney for a new life, as well as Aboriginal people who had come to live and work in the city now that their lands had been taken away.

Bungaree

★ FAMOUS FACE ★

Bungaree was born at Broken Bay, to the north of Sydney. When the British arrived, they used his skills to help them communicate with other Aboriginal groups as they sailed around the coast of Australia. Bungaree acted as a go-between to help his own community and newcomers to Australia, and often welcomed important visitors when they arrived in Sydney.

Age of youngest convict: **9**

Number of Aboriginal people living in Sydney today: **70,000**

BANGKOK

1850

CHAO PHRAYA RIVER

Bangkok, the capital of Siam (now known as Thailand), was established in 1782, when the newly crowned King Rama I decided to move the capital from one side of the river to the other to better protect it from invaders. Bangkok quickly became a city of impressive palaces and amazing temples. It was criss-crossed by a network of canals.

Field of Kings

This was originally a site for the cremation of royalty and royal ceremonies.

Wat Rakhang (Temple of Bells)

Stands on the opposite side of the river to the Grand Palace and houses five golden bells.

The Grand Palace Complex

A mini-city within the city, it contains over a hundred buildings including the Grand Palace and the Temple of the Emerald Buddha.

Wat Pho

The city's largest and oldest temple, contains a 46-metre-long golden statue of the reclining Buddha.

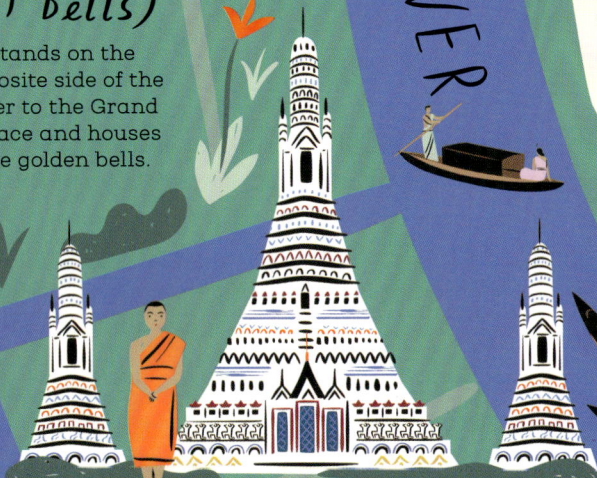

Khlong Rop Krung

Wat Arun (Temple of Dawn)

An amazing temple nearly 80 metres high, covered with colourful decorations made from glazed pieces of porcelain.

Royal Barges

Royal barges were constructed from teak wood and elaborately decorated with gold. On special occasions more than 200 barges could be on the river at the same time.

The Grand Palace Complex

Home to the king and his court, the Grand Palace complex was a mini-city within Bangkok. Materials for the construction were taken from Thon Buri on the other side of the Chao Phraya River and the destroyed old capital city of Ayutthaya.

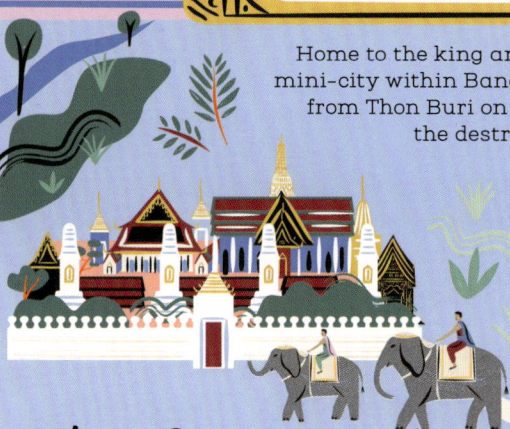

The Emerald Buddha

Carved from a solid block of green stone, it is claimed that the statue will bring good fortune to whichever kingdom possesses it.

The Grand Palace

This impressive palace was modelled on the ancient palace of Ayutthaya, in the destroyed old capital to the north.

Wat Phra Kaew

This was the most sacred temple in all of Siam and housed the Emerald Buddha.

Rattanakosin Island

THUNG PHRA MEN

The original fortress centre of Bangkok, this artificial island was created by digging a canal across a bend in the river.

Khlongs (Canals)

This system of natural and human-made waterways was used for transport throughout Bangkok.

City Walls

An impressive brick city wall was built to protect the new capital from attack.

Floating Market

Sampheng

Around half of the population in the 1850s were Chinese. This historic market district became the city's Chinatown.

LIFE IN
BANGKOK

Founded less than 250 years ago, Bangkok is one of the youngest capital cities in the world. The name Bangkok is the city's unofficial name, and refers to the little fishing village that existed on the site before it was chosen to be the new capital. It means 'village of the wild plums'. But what was life like in this brand-new capital?

City of Waterways

To move around Bangkok, people used the system of canals and waterways that flowed from the Chao Phraya River. Water taxis were the fastest way of travelling, and many people also lived in houseboats.

Bangkok's waterways also had floating markets. Colourful flowers, fresh fruit and vegetables, fabric and spices were sold from networks of small boats moored together. Each boat was packed to the brim with goods, and owners and their customers haggled for the best price.

THAILAND

Bangkok

Religious Beliefs

Religious practices were (and still are) big business in Bangkok. Many Thai people wore at least one amulet or charm featuring a picture of the Buddha or a monk for spiritual protection. Amulets are still sold in special markets, often near sacred temples.

Homes and businesses also have their own Spirit Houses, a decorated roofed structure supported by a small pillar placed in a corner of the area around the house. Offerings, such as rice, desserts, fruit and drinks, are made regularly to keep the spirits happy so that they will provide protection.

WHAT'S IN A NAME?

Thai people call Bangkok *Krung Thep* (usually translated as 'City of Angels'), which is short for the city's full ceremonial name: 'The City of Gods, the Great City, the Residence of the Emerald Buddha, the Impregnable City of the God Indra, the Grand Capital of the World Endowed with Nine Precious Gems, the Happy City Abounding in Enormous Royal Palaces which Resemble the Heavenly Abode Wherein Dwell the Reincarnated Gods, a City Given by Indra and Built by Vishvakarman' – officially the longest place name in the world!

Buddhism

Many people in Bangkok practise Theravada Buddhism, a form of the religion that developed in Southeast Asia and Sri Lanka. Monasteries also used to be schools where children were taught the moral codes of Buddhism from an early age. Boys could become novice monks from as young as seven years old.

What's in a Wat?

The city's Buddhist temples are called *Wats*, and are centres of study, medicine and religion. Wats contain images of the Buddha. The temples were often covered both inside and outside with carved, gilded, painted and inlaid decorations to honour the Buddha.

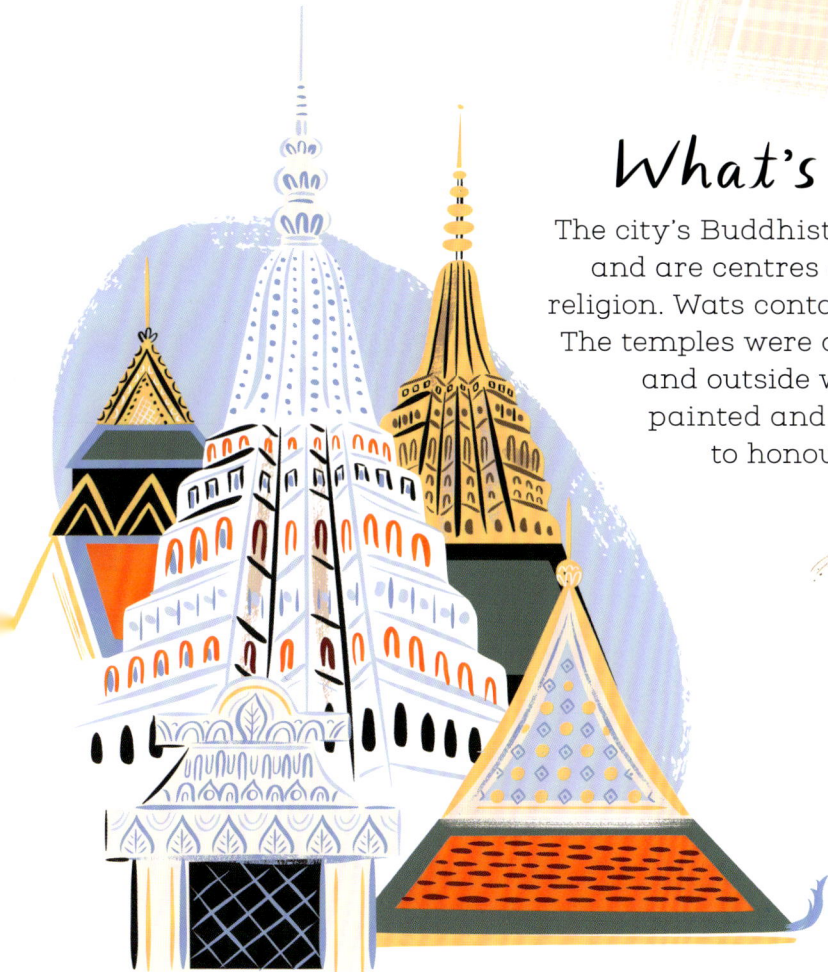

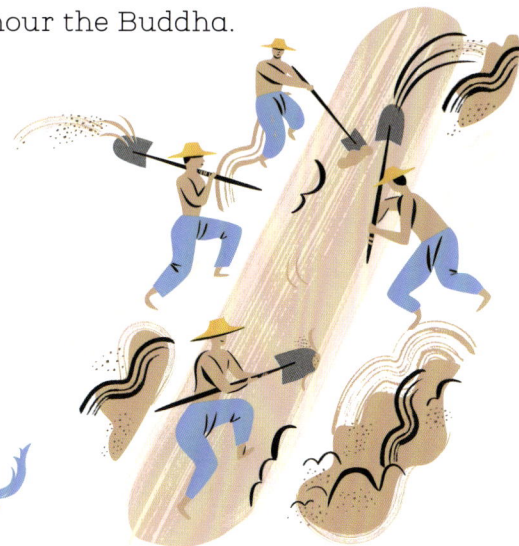

Time to Pay

At the beginning of the 1800s, ordinary workers didn't pay taxes in money – they paid in time instead. Each commoner was expected to work for the government for free for a set number of days each year. This meant that the government always had plenty of labour on hand to help build new city walls or dig new canals. As well as the labour from the tax system, the government also used enslaved people captured in wars and invasions. This system fell out of use during the 1800s.

LONDON

1880

By 1880, London, in England, had become the largest city in the world, with a population of five and a half million people. Long-reigning monarch, Queen Victoria was on the throne and Britain oversaw an empire that covered a third of the globe. London was quickly evolving into a modern city. It sat at the centre of a vast web of global trade, with goods and people arriving from and leaving for places all over the planet.

ZOO

Regent's Park

Owned by the monarch but open to the public.

Soho

A district of bars, restaurants and entertainment.

British Museum

The oldest public museum in the world.

Trafalgar Square

Large public square named to commemorate Britain's naval victory over the French at the Battle of Trafalgar in 1805. A statue of Lord Admiral Nelson, who led the fleet, stands on Nelson's Column at the centre of the square.

National Gallery

Buckingham Palace

The London residence of the British monarch has 600 rooms over three main floors. Queen Victoria was the first monarch to make this her main home.

Houses of Parliament

The home of the British (later UK) government and where Members of Parliament debate and pass new laws.

Hyde Park

SERPENTINE

Big Ben

Although the whole tower is often referred to as Big Ben, it's actually the nickname for only the clock's giant bell, which hangs within the tower and rings on the hour. The tower itself is called the 'Elizabeth Tower'.

Natural History Museum

Westminster Abbey

One of the oldest buildings in the city. Nearly every king and queen of England since 1066 CE has been crowned here.

CANAL

Victoria Park

East Londoners petitioned the queen for this 'people's park', which provided fresh air, open space and even a bathing lake for the area's overcrowded residents.

London Underground

In 1863, the world's first underground train system known as the 'Tube' was opened to the public. Gaslit wooden carriages were pulled through tunnels by steam trains.

Guildhall

East End

Many of London's slums were located in the city's east side.

St. Paul's Cathedral

This cathedral with its famous dome was finished in 1711, after the previous building was destroyed in the Great Fire of London. It was designed by Sir Christopher Wren.

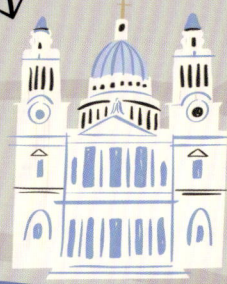

The City

The banking and financial centre of London that houses the Stock Exchange and the Bank of England.

Canals

A network of canals allowed goods to be transported across England to and from the manufacturing heartlands of the Midlands.

Tower of London

This impressive building was built by William the Conqueror in the 1070s. Over the last 900 years, the Tower has been a castle, a palace, a zoo and a prison. It is guarded by its famous Beefeaters.

83

River City

London's location near to the mouth of the River Thames helped the city become a centre of international trade.

RIVER THAMES

Borough Market

A busy and bustling market dating back to around 1014.

Southwark Cathedral

Docks

Linking with London's canals, the docks were busy with cargo being imported and exported from all over the globe.

The Great Stink

For years, untreated human waste flowed into the Thames, causing outbreaks of disease, which killed thousands of people. During one particularly hot summer in 1858, the smell finally became too much for Londoners to bear. 'The Great Stink' made the city authorities realise something had to be done. Engineer Joseph Bazalgette proposed a new sewer system.

Shipyards

Once a major industry, by 1880 only a few survived.

Number of London Underground stations in 1880:

49

Number of London Underground stations today:

270

Population of London in 1880:

5.5
million

Population of London today:

8.5
million

LIFE IN LONDON

London, the capital city of England, grew enormously during the reign of Queen Victoria, a time known as the 'Victorian age'. The city expanded from a population of just one million in 1800 to over six million by the end of the century. It was a time of huge change not only for the city itself but also in the way many Londoners lived their daily lives.

London's Slums

Parts of London were dirty, dangerous and full of diseases. Thousands of poor people lived in terrible conditions in slums, which were overcrowded neighbourhoods crammed with leaky, cold and unsafe houses. Many of the worst slums were in East London, where whole families often lived cramped together in one room. Sickness and disease were a constant threat and were increased by the overcrowding and damp conditions.

No Picnic

For many children in 1880s London, life was tough. Really tough. Recently, laws had been passed saying that all children aged between five and 13 had to go to school, but it was not free. It cost at least a penny a week to send a child to school and for many poor families this was too much. Many children were expected to help earn money and worked long, hard hours selling flowers, fruit or matches on the street in all weathers.

★ FAMOUS FACE ★

Queen Victoria ruled for 64 years, from 1837 to 1901, and oversaw more change during her long reign than probably any other monarch. She was involved in the affairs and decisions of state while overseeing her large family. After her husband, Albert, died, in 1860, Victoria went into a long period of mourning and was seen much less often by her subjects.

Queen Victoria

UNITED KINGDOM

London

Getting on Track

By 1880, the railways had had a huge impact on London and the lives of the people there. A growing network of railway lines linked the capital with the rest of the country. In London itself, the world's first underground railway had opened, making fast, safe, affordable travel available to many more people. Passengers in carriages were pulled through underground tunnels by coal-powered steam engines belching out thick smoke, making for rather noisy and dirty journeys!

Sound of the Suburbs

The new railways meant that people could work in the middle of the city, and commute in and out each day. This led to the rise of the suburbs, residential areas on the edge of cities and towns consisting mostly of homes. The suburbs were less overcrowded and less dirty than the city centres. Suburban houses could be larger with bigger gardens because there was more space. This was the way that London and other world cities grew – not only because of more people coming to live and work in them but also by expanding to swallow up the countryside around them.

SAINT PETERSBURG

1917

On the bitterly cold night of 7 November 1917, events occurred in the Russian city of Saint Petersburg (then called Petrograd) that changed the world forever. After decades of wars, famine and bad treatment by the ruling tsar, or emperor, thousands of unhappy workers had risen up in revolution. Following months of violent protests, a small political party called the Bolsheviks stormed the Winter Palace, the seat of the Russian national government. They easily overpowered the few guards in the building, and the world saw the birth of what would become the Soviet Union.

GULF OF FINLAND

SMOLENKA RIVER

Old Saint Petersburg Stock Exchange and Rostral Columns

Founded by Peter the Great and built between 1805 and 1810.

Vasilyevsky Island

An island on which many of Saint Petersburg's most historic buildings stand. The eastern section is built in a grid pattern.

Saint Andrew's Cathedral

MOYKA

Peterhof Palace
↙ 36 km Southwest

A group of stunning palaces and gardens in Peterhof, on the Gulf of Finland near Saint Petersburg. It was built by Peter the Great as Russia's answer to the Palace of Versailles in Paris.

FURTHER SOUTH

Putilov Ironworks

A huge metal-working factory. In 1904, four ironworkers lost their jobs. Early the next year, their fellow workers decided to strike. This was one of the first events that led to the larger protests in the city.

Grand Choral Synagogue

The third largest synagogue in Europe.

KARPOVKA RIVER

BOLSHAYA NEVKA RIVER

Peter and Paul Cathedral

Russian Orthodox cathedral located inside the fortress. Its gold spire is topped by an angel holding a cross – an important symbol of the city. Most Russian tsars and empresses are buried here, including Catherine the Great.

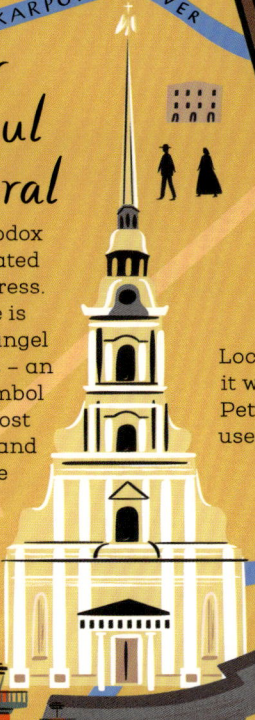

Peter and Paul Fortress

Located on Zayachy Island, it was built as a fortress by Peter the Great in 1703, but used as a prison for most of its working life.

Finland Station

Steam trains left from here, linking Russia with Finland.

NEVA RIVER

Flows through Saint Petersburg into the Gulf of Finland.

Zayachy Island

Also known as Hare Island. Much of this area was swampland reclaimed for use by the city.

Menshikov Palace

Built in 1710, this was the first stone building in the city.

Hermitage Museum

Large museum with its collections spread across six buildings, including the Winter Palace. Its three million objects include the largest collection of paintings in the world.

Palace Square

Central city square and site of the 'Bloody Sunday' massacre.

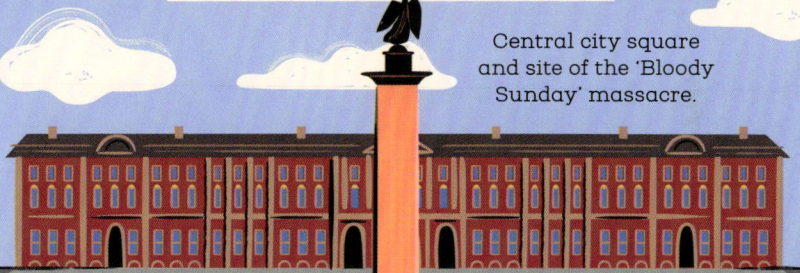

The Winter Palace

The official residence of the Russian tsars from 1762 to 1917. After the revolution it was used to house collections from the Hermitage Museum.

Alexander Column

Made from a single piece of carved red granite and said to be the tallest column of its kind in the world. It commemorates the Russian victory over Napoleon's France.

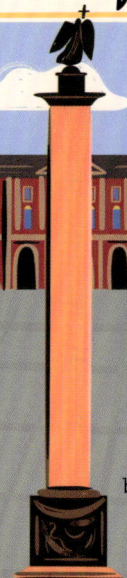

RIVER

Admiralty Building

Headquarters of the Imperial Russian Navy. Its spire is topped by a gold weathervane in the form of a warship.

FONTANKA RIVER

Trinity Cathedral

Also known as Troitsky Cathedral. It is 80 metres tall and large enough inside for 3,000 worshippers.

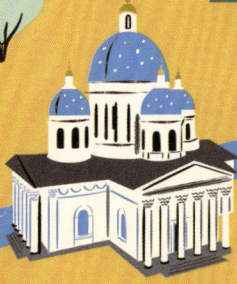

Nevsky Prospekt

This main street in Saint Petersburg is where tens of thousands of women marched for the right to vote.

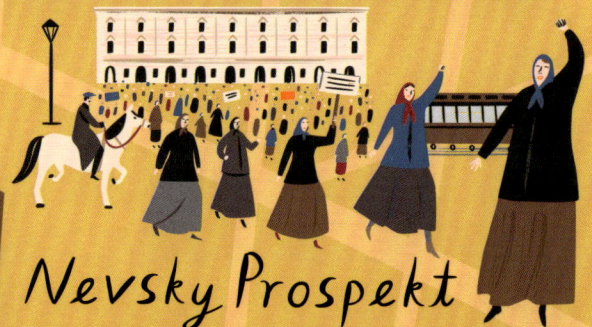

LIFE IN SAINT PETERSBURG

Saint Petersburg was founded in 1703 by the Russian tsar, Peter the Great. He wanted Russia to become a great trading nation. He knew that to become a true international power, Russia needed a seaport that faced Europe. So, he created the new city of Saint Petersburg on barren marshland, using 'serfs' from the local countryside. They were forced to drain the swamps and drive building piles into the ground. Many lost their lives in terrible conditions.

Saint Petersburg

RUSSIA

White Nights

The summer in Saint Petersburg is famous for its 'White Nights'. The city's northern location means that the sun doesn't set between the months of May and July, so it never gets completely dark. In the dead of night, the sun sits low in the sky, giving the city streets a pearly white glow.

Too Big for Comfort

In 1917, the Russian Empire was huge, covering one-sixth of the land surface of the entire planet. (Only two other empires have ever been bigger – the Mongol and the British.) It stretched from the western border with Germany all the way to the Pacific Ocean in the east, 8,000 kilometres away! Its population was around 164 million, of which 80 per cent were peasants, people who farmed land for the wealthy landowners.

Not Pleasant for a Peasant

If you were a worker or a peasant in Russia in 1917, then life was hard indeed. Poor people lived in terrible conditions in both the countryside and cities. In the countryside, peasants were often treated no better than the animals. In cities like Saint Petersburg, it was not uncommon for up to 15 workers to share one smelly, damp apartment. Rooms would smell very bad because of the mixture of dirt, rubbish and sewage from the outside streets. Workers were terribly paid, never earning enough money to escape poverty. Saint Petersburg had many soup kitchens that helped the poor survive.

SAINT PETERSBURG IN NUMBERS

Number of serfs who built the city over the first 18 years:

About 540,000

Hours a serf worked each week:

Around

★ FAMOUS FACE ★

Lenin (real name Vladimir Ilich Ulyanov) was the leader of the Bolshevik Revolution and later became the first head of the Soviet state. He is regarded as one of the most important thinkers of the twentieth century. He lived in Saint Petersburg before being exiled to Siberia, travelling to Europe once his exile had ended. He returned to Russia in October 1917, arriving at Saint Petersburg's Finland Station on a sealed train. Some stories say he was even disguised as a railway worker!

Lenin

Bloody Sunday

In 1905, a strike by workers at the Putilov Ironworks led to a confrontation in which over 100 people were shot and killed by government troops. This was called 'Bloody Sunday'. It inspired similar strikes across the country and increased resentment towards the tsar and the ruling classes.

The End of an Era

In 1918, the capital of Russia was changed to Moscow, 600 kilometres to the southeast of Saint Petersburg. One reason for this was that the capital was now much further away from Russia's borders, making it harder to invade in the event of war.

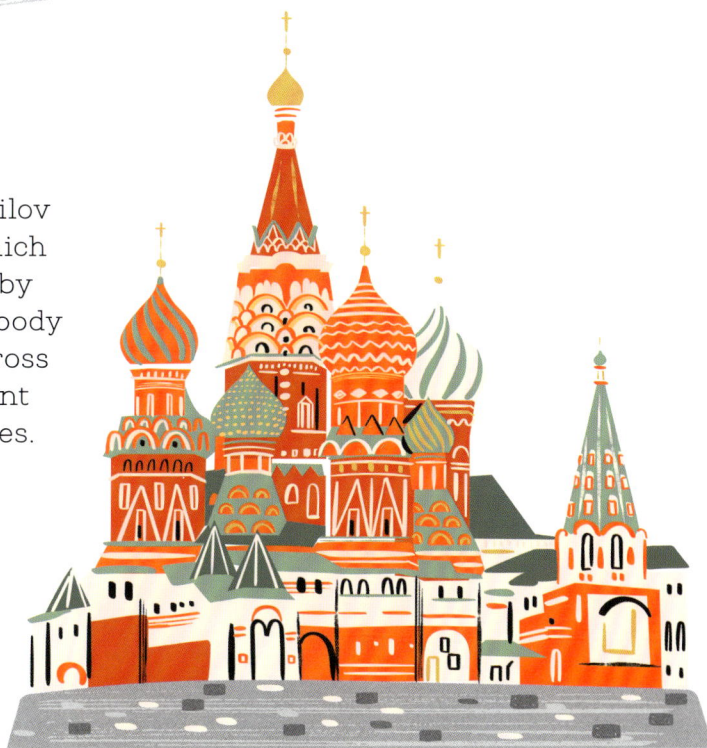

66 Population of Saint Petersburg in 1917: **2.5** million

Population of Saint Petersburg today: **5.5** million

NEW YORK CITY

1931

Almost a century ago, New York City was busy getting taller. Business was booming and so was the population: every year, tens of thousands of people arrived from all over the world in search of a better life. Space was limited, so people started to build upwards instead of outwards. The incredible skyscrapers of New York changed the way that cities would be built forever.

HUDSON

← NEW JERSEY

Ellis Island

Where people arriving in America were registered, interviewed and examined to check they were healthy, before starting their new lives.

Piers

Hell's Kitchen

Times Square

Originally called Longacre Square, it was renamed after the *New York Times* newspaper in 1904.

PLANTERS PEANUTS   BROADWAY

Statue of Liberty

A gift from the people of France, this symbol of freedom has welcomed people to New York since 1886.

Whitney Museum

SUBWAY

Singer Building

New York Central Railroad

High Line

Woolworth Building

Washington Square Park

Flatiron Building

STATEN ISLAND ↙

New York World Building

Gramercy Park

Wall Street

Many banks were built on and around Wall Street. New York was (and still is) America's financial centre.

Lower East Side

This area was full of crowded high-rise apartment blocks known as tenement buildings. Many new immigrants and their families lived in this area.

Financial District

Battery Park

EAST RIVER

New York Harbour

One of the world's largest natural harbours, this was the perfect place for ships to unload goods and passengers from all over the world.

Brooklyn Bridge

CHOP SUEY

Chinatown

Williamsburg Bridge

Manhattan Bridge

BROOKLYN ↓

90

RIVER

Riverside Park

Grant's Tomb

Columbia University

Harlem
200,000 African Americans came to live here in the 1920s.

Upper West Side

Central Park
Built in the 1800s, this is now one of the most famous parks in the world.

Empire State Building
This was the world's tallest building for more than 40 years.

New York and Harlem Railroad

HARLEM RIVER

Yankee Stadium

Upper East Side

MANHATTAN

THE BRONX

Metropolitan Museum of Art

Chrysler Building

MoMA

Bryant Park

Garment District

New York Public Library

Diamond District

Originally called 'New Amsterdam', the city of New York began on Manhattan island.

TAXI

FRANKFURTERS 5¢

Gracie Mansion

RANDALL'S ISLAND

91

LOANS

GROCERY

WELFARE ISLAND

Queensboro Bridge

Astoria Park

Manhattan is one of five boroughs that make up New York City. The others are:

Brooklyn, Queens, Staten Island and the Bronx.

The boroughs were united into one city in 1898.

QUEENS

Long Island City

DINER

LIFE IN NEW YORK CITY

UNITED STATES of AMERICA

New York City

The 1920s were a time of excitement and glamour in New York – for some people at least. Businesses were making a lot of people very rich at a time when New York had more people living in it than any other city in the world.

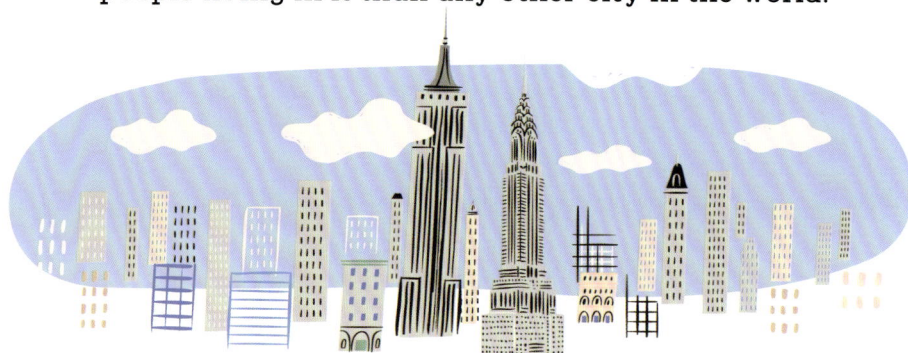

A City in the Clouds

Business owners had more money than ever before, and new inventions such as electric lifts and concrete and metal-framed buildings meant that more and more skyscrapers were built. Two buildings raced to the top of Manhattan's skyline in the 1920s. The Chrysler building, finished in 1930, was the world's tallest building . . . until the following year. The Empire State Building, which was completed in 1931, remained the world's tallest building for 40 years!

Neighbours from All Over the World

Many immigrants to New York ended up living in Manhattan's Lower East Side, creating communities such as 'Little Italy' and 'Chinatown'. Poorer families often lived, ate and slept together in just one room, in a kind of high-rise apartment block known as a tenement building.

During the 1920s, hundreds of thousands of African Americans from the southern states also came to New York City, looking for better job opportunities. Many went to live in Harlem, and the jazz and blues music they brought with them became wildly popular, so that the 1920s became known as the 'Jazz Age'.

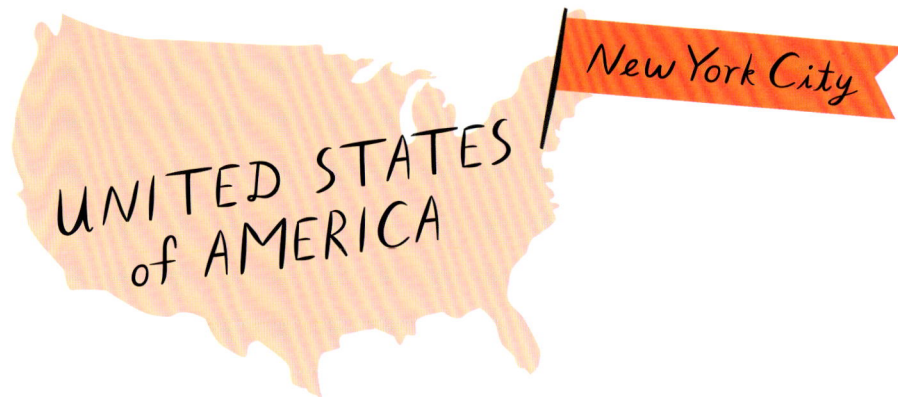

The First New Yorkers

By the 1930s, immigrants had been arriving in New York for over 300 years. The first were the Dutch, who arrived in the 1600s when a tribe of 20,000 Native American Lenape people hunted and farmed in the region. They were gradually forced out, first by the European settlers and finally by the government. Many Lenape people now live in Oklahoma.

Fun and Freedom

Amazing new inventions, such as washing machines and refrigerators, meant that well-off people had more time for fun activities – such as listening to jazz on the newly invented wireless radio or on record players. More people now had money to buy luxuries, including cars, fashionable clothes and make-up. American women won the right to vote in 1920, and with many more girls finishing school, women began to have more freedom to choose how they lived.

Bleecker Street BAKERY

The Great Depression

Everything changed when New York's stock market crashed in 1929, causing 10 years of financial problems known as the 'Great Depression'. During this time, companies went out of business and millions lost their jobs across the United States. Many of the hardest hit families ended up homeless, and people from all walks of life queued for hours for stale bread so they could save their families from starving to death.

★ FAMOUS FACE ★

Zora Neale Hurston was an African-American woman from the southern states, who moved to New York City in the 1920s. She studied anthropology at Barnard College (part of Columbia University), where she was the only black student, and went on to become a writer, celebrating African-American culture in her novels.

THEIR EYES WERE WATCHING GOD

Zora Neale Hurston

NEW YORK CITY IN NUMBERS

Height of the tallest skyscraper in 1931:

381

metres

Empire State Building

Height of the tallest skyscraper today:

541

metres

One World Trade Center

Population of New York City in the 1920s:

5.6

million

Population of New York City today:

8.6

million

BERLIN

At the end of the Second World War, the German capital, Berlin, became a divided city. Some parts of it were left in the control of the Western Allies (the United Kingdom, France and the United States) as part of West Germany. However, the rest was controlled by the Soviet Union and became part of East Germany. This meant that the little section of West Germany in Berlin was surrounded by Soviet-controlled East Germany. To prevent people moving from poorer East Germany to the richer West, a wall was built completely enclosing West Berlin. The Berlin Wall became a symbol of the 'Iron Curtain' between the forces of the West and the Soviets.

94

The Reichstag

Built as a home for the German Parliament. It was burned down in an arson attack in the 1930s and fell into ruin after the Second World War. It was partly reconstructed between 1961 and 1964, but was not used again as the seat of government until many years later, after German reunification – when West Germany and East Germany became one country again in 1990.

Berlin Zoological Garden

This famous zoo opened in 1844.

Brandenburg Gate

Built between 1788 and 1791, this has been the backdrop to many historic events. It has come to be an important symbol of European unity and peace.

Kaiser-Wilhelm-Gedächtniskirche (Kaiser Wilhelm Memorial Church)

One of the city's most famous landmarks. This church was destroyed by bombs in the Second World War. The church building was rebuilt, but the damaged spire of the old church was left as a monument to the conflict.

BRITISH

RIVER HAVEL

Death Strip

An empty, exposed area between the east and west sides of the wall. It allowed guards to easily see off any attempted escape.

Checkpoint Bravo

The main road border crossing between West Berlin and East Germany.

The Berlin Wall

EAST

WEST

This was a barrier that enclosed West Berlin and stopped people crossing the border from East to West. Along the wall were watchtowers, manned by guards armed with machine guns.

FRENCH SECTOR

Tiergarten

The city's central park, running west from the Brandenburg Gate. It includes the Berlin Zoological Garden and the Berlin Victory Column.

Ministry for State Security

Home to the East German Secret Police, known as the Stasi. Their job was to make sure the East Germans did as they were told.

Schloss Charlottenburg

A royal palace originally built between 1695 and 1699, and famous for its fantastically decorated rooms.

Alexanderplatz

A large public square known to locals simply as 'Alex'.

SECTOR

AMERICAN SECTOR

YOU ARE LEAVING THE AMERICAN SECTOR

Checkpoint Charlie

This was the main crossover point for westerners between East and West Berlin. It became a symbol of the 'Cold War' between the Soviet Union and the West.

RIVER SPREE

Karl-Marx-Allee

A mile-long shopping boulevard containing shops, bars, restaurants and a huge cinema. It was East Germany's 'flagship' building project.

SOVIET SECTOR

Tempelhof Airport

Once West Berlin's central airport. It was the site of the famous 'Berlin Airlift' (1948–9), when vital supplies were flown into blockaded West Berlin from the 'mainland' of West Germany.

A Divided City

The Berlin Wall was 156 kilometres long and over three metres high. On the East German side, a second fence was built 100 metres away from the main wall running exactly parallel. Buildings between the two walls were demolished, leaving a flat, barren area known as the 'Death Strip'. The empty area gave guards a clear line of fire at anyone who entered. The surface was sand or gravel, making footprints easier to see. Trenches were dug to stop escapes by vehicle.

BERLIN
IN NUMBERS

Number of people who tried to escape across the Berlin Wall (1961 to 1989):

Up to

100,000

Number of people who actually escaped:

Around

8,000

Population of Berlin in 1964:

3.2 million

Population of Berlin today:

3.6 million

LIFE IN
BERLIN

Berlin

GERMANY

Berlin was a unique city, with control split between the Allies in the West and the Soviets in the East. It became an important border in the long rivalry between the West and the Soviet Union, known as the Cold War. Because of this, Berlin has been used as the backdrop for many thrilling spy stories in books, films and on TV.

Escape

People found many ingenious and not so ingenious ways to try and get over the Wall to freedom. In the early days, some people jumped from buildings next to the Wall to get over it, some dug long tunnels underneath it and a few even slid along wires from one side to the other. One enterprising individual, Wolfgang Engels, stole an armoured personnel carrier and tried to drive it through the Wall. His vehicle crashed but even though he was shot by East German border guards, he survived and started a new life in West Germany.

The Stasi

People in East Berlin lived in fear of the Stasi, the East German secret police. It was the Stasi's job to ensure that the citizens of East Germany (including East Berlin) remained loyal to the state. The Stasi were based in the huge Ministry for State Security in East Berlin. They went to great lengths to spy on their own population, looking for people about to 'defect' and leave East Germany. Phone calls were recorded, homes were bugged with listening devices and secret spy cameras were used to find out what people were up to. Many people were informants for the Stasi, and some were even paid to give information on their fellow citizens.

The Berlin Airlift

In 1948, the Soviet Union decided to blockade the West German part of Berlin. The blockade stopped all food, fuel and other supplies from arriving by road and rail. West Berlin had only 36 days' worth of food in reserve. The Western Allies responded with one of the biggest ever airlifts, using aircraft to fly supplies directly into Tempelhof Airport. At the peak of the airlift, one plane arrived every 30 seconds! One enterprising pilot, who became known as the 'Berlin Candy Bomber', even dropped sweets carried by miniature parachutes to the city's children. West Berlin was kept supplied with food and the Soviets ended their blockade nine months later.

Life with the Wall

The Berlin Wall not only split the city, but it split up family and friends as well. Living conditions were very different on the two sides of the Wall. In the western section of the city, shops had food and goods imported from the West, while in the East German section consumers had much less choice of things they could buy. Here too, it was forbidden to play rock 'n' roll music in public, and people weren't even allowed to dance in styles popular in the West.

★ FAMOUS FACE ★

A few months after the Berlin Wall went up, railway worker Harry Deterling spotted a disused track that led to West Berlin. Harry loaded a train with his family and friends and, on 5 December 1961, drove 'the last train to freedom' towards a new life in the West. Scattering surprised border guards, their escape was successful. The East German police sealed off the route the next day.

Harry Deterling

The End of an Era

In the late 1980s, a series of revolutions in other countries under Soviet control spilled over into East Germany. East German border guards were overwhelmed by the numbers of protesters arriving on the eastern side of the Wall. The authorities reluctantly had to allow free passage from East Berlin to West Berlin. Celebrating crowds soon gathered and started to climb onto and over the Berlin Wall. After 28 years of dividing a city, the Berlin Wall had fallen.

SAN FRANCISCO

2010s

San Francisco is a modern city world-famous for its culture and never-say-die attitude, and set against the beautiful San Francisco Bay Area. The city is known for its trams, hills, summer fogs and stunning Golden Gate Bridge. The Bay Area is now also the location of Silicon Valley – the technology centre of the USA, leading the way into the future.

Golden Gate National Recreation Area

One of the largest and most visited urban parks in the world.

PACIFIC OCEAN

The largest and deepest ocean on Earth.

SAN ANDREAS FAULT

SAN FRANCISCO BAY

San Andreas Fault

Earthquake-causing fault line that runs near to the city. Minor earthquakes happen frequently with much more powerful quakes every century or so. A large earthquake is now overdue.

SILICON VALLEY

Sitting south of the city of San Francisco is Silicon Valley, the centre of the computer and technology industries in the USA.

Facebook World HQ

Located in the nearby city of Menlo Park. Facebook Inc. owns WhatsApp and Instagram and is one of the most valuable companies in the world.

Googleplex

The HQ of the multinational technology company Google is in nearby Mountain View.

California Redwoods

These evergreens are some of the Earth's tallest, and oldest, trees.

Apple Park

The headquarters of computer company Apple is located in nearby Cupertino. It is nicknamed the 'Spaceship' because of its futuristic design, including a roof covered in solar panels. Inside the 'doughnut' is a park.

Sunset District

AROUND THE BAY

Golden Gate Bridge

One of the most famous and photographed suspension bridges in the world. It opened to traffic in 1937. Its main span is 1,280 metres and its towers rise to 227 metres above the water of the bay.

Alcatraz Island

Once home to Alcatraz Federal Penitentiary, one of the toughest prisons in the world. It closed in 1963 and the island is now a museum.

SAN FRANCISCO BAY

One of California's most important ecological habitats and home to many species of wildlife.

Treasure Island

An artificially constructed island connected by a 270-metre causeway to Yerba Buena Island.

101

Presidio National Park

A park and former military fort. Offers woods, hills and amazing views.

Fisherman's Wharf

A well-known tourist attraction that includes museums, shops, bars and restaurants.

Russian and Nob Hills

Two of San Francisco's many hills with amazing views over the city and bay.

Financial District

Contains the headquarters of many important banks, as well as firms like Twitter, Uber and Lyft.

Cable Car Network

Providing an easy way up and down the city's many hills.

THRIFT

①

BOOKS

Chinatown

Dating back to 1850. Pagoda-style roofs and dragon lanterns line the streets in this top tourist attraction.

80

DIM SUM

TACOS

Painted Ladies

A row of colourful Victorian houses.

Haight-Ashbury District

Buena Vista Park

Golden Gate Park

Castro District

One of the first openly LGBT+ neighbourhoods in the world.

SOURDOUGH

CAFE

BREWERY

Mission District

Before the arrival of the Spanish missionaries who gave the 'Mission' its name, this area was home to the Ohlone people, who populated much of the San Francisco Bay Area.

LIFE IN
SAN FRANCISCO

The citizens of San Francisco rightly enjoy a reputation for being freethinking. The city was central to the birth of the hippie counterculture movement in the 1960s, as well as contributing to the peace movement, and the gay rights movement. But like most big cities, San Francisco has issues with homelessness and wage inequalities between the best- and worst-paid people.

San Francisco,
UNITED STATES
of AMERICA

Going for Gold

San Francisco Chronicle
GOLD RUSH!
Gold in the Hills

In its very early days, the population of San Francisco grew quickly because of the California Gold Rush. People arrived from all over the world, hoping to dig up gold and get rich quick. Between 1848 and the end of 1849, the population jumped from 1,000 to 20,000 people, displacing many of the Ohlone people, the original indigenous inhabitants of the region. The greed for gold was so strong that hundreds of ships lay abandoned in the harbour as their crews headed to the hills to seek treasure! Some of the ships were converted and used as floating bars and hotels before they eventually rotted and sank.

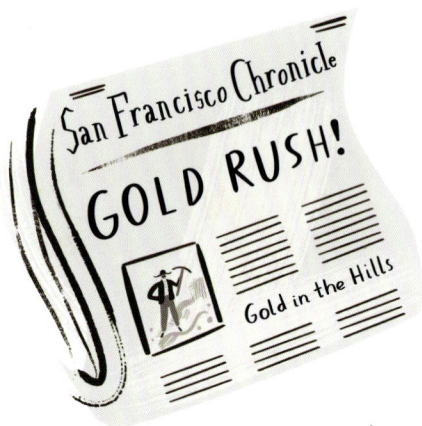

★ FAMOUS FACE ★

Harvey Milk was a resident of the Castro District and the first openly gay elected official in California. He was an activist in the 1970s and made enormous strides for gay rights, including sponsoring a bill banning discrimination on the basis of sexual orientation. He was assassinated in 1978.

Harvey Milk

Earthquake, Death and Destruction!

San Francisco is built close to the San Andreas Fault, an area where two plates of the Earth's crust move past each other, causing regular earth tremors. On 18 April 1906, the thriving city was hit by an enormous earthquake. For around a minute, the ground moved, shaking apart the city's buildings and reducing many to ruins.

To try and stop the resulting fires spreading through the damaged buildings, whole city blocks were blown up using gunpowder, to create a firebreak to stop the flames. Unfortunately, the explosions started many new fires and made the situation worse. The city burned for three days, 3,000 people died and over 250,000 people lost their homes. However, the city soon began to be rebuilt, rising out of the ashes with new, safer buildings.

High-tech Home

Silicon Valley is located in the southern part of the San Francisco Bay Area and is famous around the world for its computer and technology companies.

Many of the biggest in the world are located there or nearby, including names like Apple, Facebook, Google, Netflix, Paypal, Twitter and many more. As well as huge multinational companies, the area is home to thousands of smaller 'start-up' companies, all hoping for a bright future selling their new technology.

Tall Tales

The Bay Area is home to some of the most fantastic trees on the planet, called Redwoods. These giants of nature can grow to be over 100 metres tall and are the tallest trees in the world. Some of the Coast Redwoods here have been proven to be over 2,000 years old. They were cut down for timber in the past, but many that remain are now protected in National Parks.

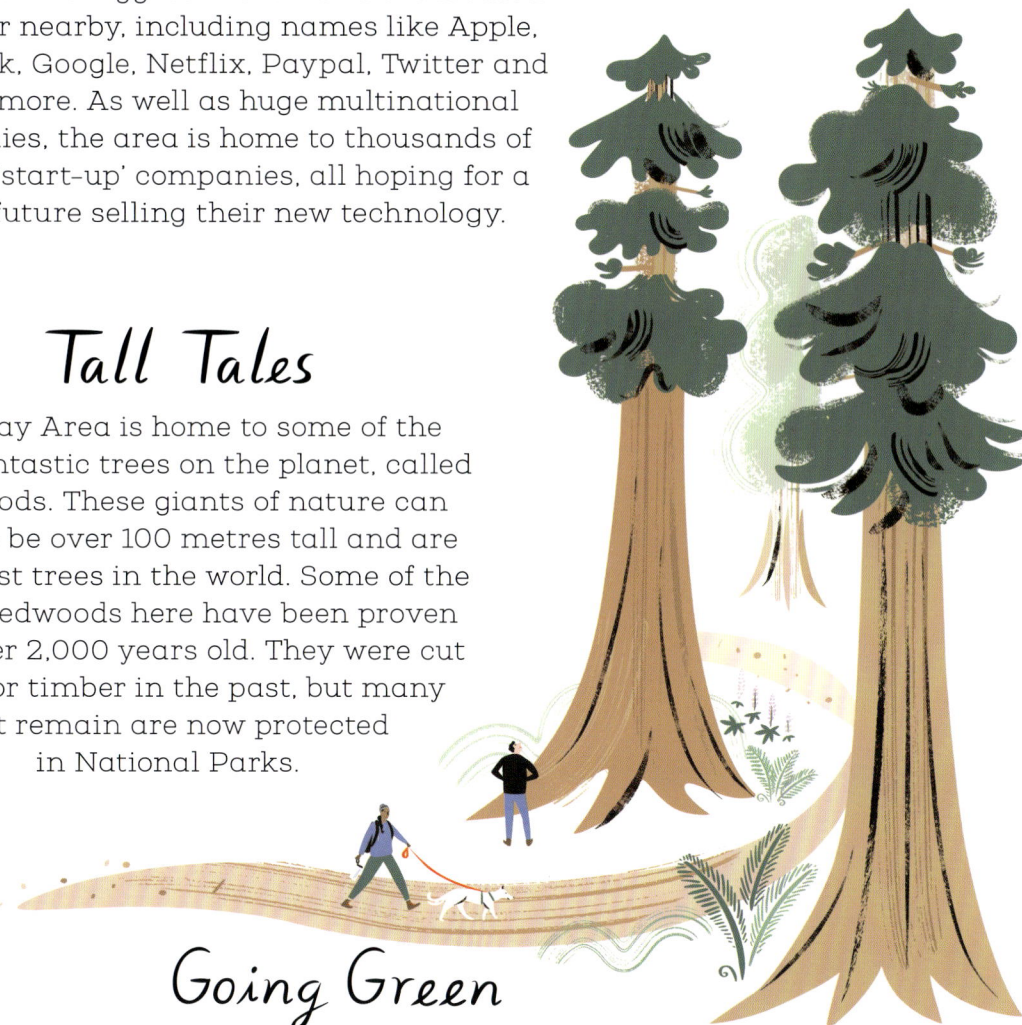

Going Green

San Francisco is a city with environmental concerns at its heart. It often leads the way on important issues like recycling and solar power, and its parks and green spaces are celebrated. One area of concern is the shallow San Francisco Bay. Fishing and pollution have damaged its fragile ecosystem. Now it's being protected and helped to recover.

SAN FRANCISCO IN NUMBERS

Number of hills in the city:

48

Lowest point in the city:

0 metres

Highest point in the city:

Mount Davidson at

283 metres

Percentage of the city destroyed by earthquake and fire in 1906:

80%

Population of San Francisco today:

880,000

TOKYO

TODAY

Originally a small fishing village, Tokyo has grown to become the busy, colourful capital of Japan. A city of contrasts, with neon-lit glass skyscrapers next to ancient wooden shrines, Tokyo is now home to more people than any other city on Earth.

Mode Gakuen Cocoon Tower

Tokyo Metropolitan Government Building

The huge Tokyo area is governed from here.

Meiji Jingū

Japan has two major religions: Shintō and Buddhism. This is a Shintō shrine.

Shinjuku Station

The busiest railway station in the world. Stations employ 'pushers', who literally push people on to crowded trains during rush hour.

Shinjuku Gyoen

People gather here for the cherry blossom festival every spring – there are more than 1,500 cherry trees.

Imperial Palace

The Emperor of Japan's home. The palace stands in beautiful gardens, and includes Edo Castle, first built in 1457.

Iceberg Building

Zōjōji Temple

Tokyo Tower

Inspired by the Eiffel Tower in Paris, this tower was built in 1958. The top is slightly bent after an earthquake in 2011.

Minato City

Shibuya Crossing

In rush hour, 2,500 people might be crossing this road junction at any one time!

Mount Fuji

↙ 99 km Southwest

The highest mountain in Japan and an active volcano. Mount Fuji last erupted in 1707.

Ueno Park

Many museums, galleries, temples, shrines and even a zoo are found here.

ZOO

Sensōji Temple

Tokyo's oldest Buddhist temple, first built nearly 1,400 years ago.

Tokyo Skytree

The tallest tower in the world at 634 metres tall.

Sumida

Akihabara

This area is famous for video gaming, anime and manga.

SUMIDA RIVER

Bank of Japan

Chiyoda

Ginza

Tokyo's most famous shopping district.

The Heart of Japan

The Greater Tokyo Area is vast and includes islands in the Philippine Sea that are 1,850 kilometres away from the city centre. Tokyo is on the largest of Japan's islands, Honshu.

103

Chūō

The central district of Tokyo. On a working day, this area contains more than 60,000 people per square kilometre!

Hamarikyu Gardens

TOKYO'S 23 WARDS

Tokyo is split up into areas called 'wards'.

TOKYO BAY

Rainbow Bridge

Toyosu Fish Market

Home to the biggest seafood market in the world.

LIFE IN TOKYO

Tokyo has been devastated and risen from the ashes twice in the last 100 years. As a result, it's now one of the most modern high-rise cities on the planet, gleaming with tall glass buildings by day and alight with bright colours at night.

JAPAN | Tokyo

From Village to Metropolis

Originally a small fishing village called Edo, by 1721 the city was home to over a million people and the biggest city in the world. In 1868, Emperor Meiji moved from the old capital of Japan, Kyōto, and changed the name of his new capital from Edo to Tokyo.

The city lay in ruins twice in the twentieth century: in 1923 Tokyo was destroyed by an earthquake, and in the Second World War it was heavily bombed. Yet by the 1960s, Tokyo was the first ever city to have more than 10 million people living in it.

Kawaii

Kawaii means 'cute' or 'adorable', but in Japan it's a way of life. Everything can be *kawaii*, from doughnuts to backpacks. In Tokyo there are kawaii shops and cafés that offer unbounded cuteness, packed with brightly coloured images of baby animals, mythical creatures and teddy bears.

TOKYO IN NUMBERS

Size of the Greater Tokyo Area:

13,000 square kilometres

Percentage of people in Japan who live in Tokyo: **25%**

WHAT'S IN A NAME?

According to Japanese tradition, babies are named at a ceremony when they are seven days old. Popular Japanese names are Hana for a girl and Haruto for a boy, but names are complicated because they can be spelled differently and have different meanings in *kanji* (Japanese writing). On their first birthday, babies hold a special rice cake with their name written on it as a symbol that they'll always be healthy, happy and have plenty of food in the future.

HELLO my name is **Haruto**

★ FAMOUS FACE ★

Hayao Miyazaki is a writer, animator and manga artist who is most famous for his anime feature films. He was born and still lives in Tokyo, where his animation studio, Studio Ghibli, is based.

Hayao Miyazaki

The Ring of Fire

Japan lies on the edge of one of the huge plates in the Earth's crust, which means that there's a risk of earthquakes and volcanic eruptions. In fact, the islands of Japan are made from erupting volcanoes – the latest island appeared in 2013! Mount Fuji is an active volcano but hasn't erupted for hundreds of years.

Earthquakes are always a threat. New buildings are built to withstand quakes, and everyone knows what to do if the ground starts to shake – children have earthquake drills at school. During these practice sessions, they wear protective fabric helmets and hide under their desks. The last big earthquake was in 2011, just off the coast of northeast Japan, which was the fifth-strongest recorded earthquake in history.

Population of central Tokyo: **9.2** million

Population of the Greater Tokyo Area: **38** million

CITIES of TODAY

Thousands of years ago, the first cities brought together large numbers of people, helping them to survive by sharing resources. Since then, cities have evolved into exciting places to live. People are drawn to them because there are jobs, activities and lots and lots of other people. Today, cities around the world represent the best of humanity's achievements, but also many of our failings.

Over the last 10,000 years, more and more people have been coming to live in cities. By 1800, about seven people in every hundred lived in cities. Today, more than half of us live in them. By 2050, it is estimated that at least two out of three people will be city dwellers.

Driving into Trouble

Many of the cars, buses and lorries that keep today's cities moving are driven by coal, oil and gas – fossil fuels – which release carbon dioxide into the atmosphere. This extra carbon dioxide created by the way we live is causing climate change. The world's temperature is rising, causing ice to melt at the North and South Poles, making the sea level rise and creating extreme weather conditions.

Energy Hogs

Cities take up less than two per cent of the world's land, yet they consume more than two thirds of its energy and produce more than 70 per cent of its carbon dioxide emissions. Now, and in the future, cities will need to change in order to help counter global warming.

GARAGE

BANK

Market

LAUNDRY

Vanishing Islands

Many cities are also at risk from rising sea levels. Most in danger is Malé, the capital city of the Maldives, which is a country made up of more than 1,000 islands in the Indian Ocean. The highest island in the Maldives is only just over two metres above sea level. A new island is being created near Malé by pumping sand into the ocean to make a foundation to build on, protected by three-metre-high walls.

Sinking Cities

Around the world, lots of other cities could be flooded as sea levels rise. The biggest is Shanghai in China, but there are many more: Miami in the United States, Venice in Italy, Rio de Janeiro in Brazil, Dhaka in Bangladesh, Jakarta in Indonesia and Lagos in Nigeria are all in danger.

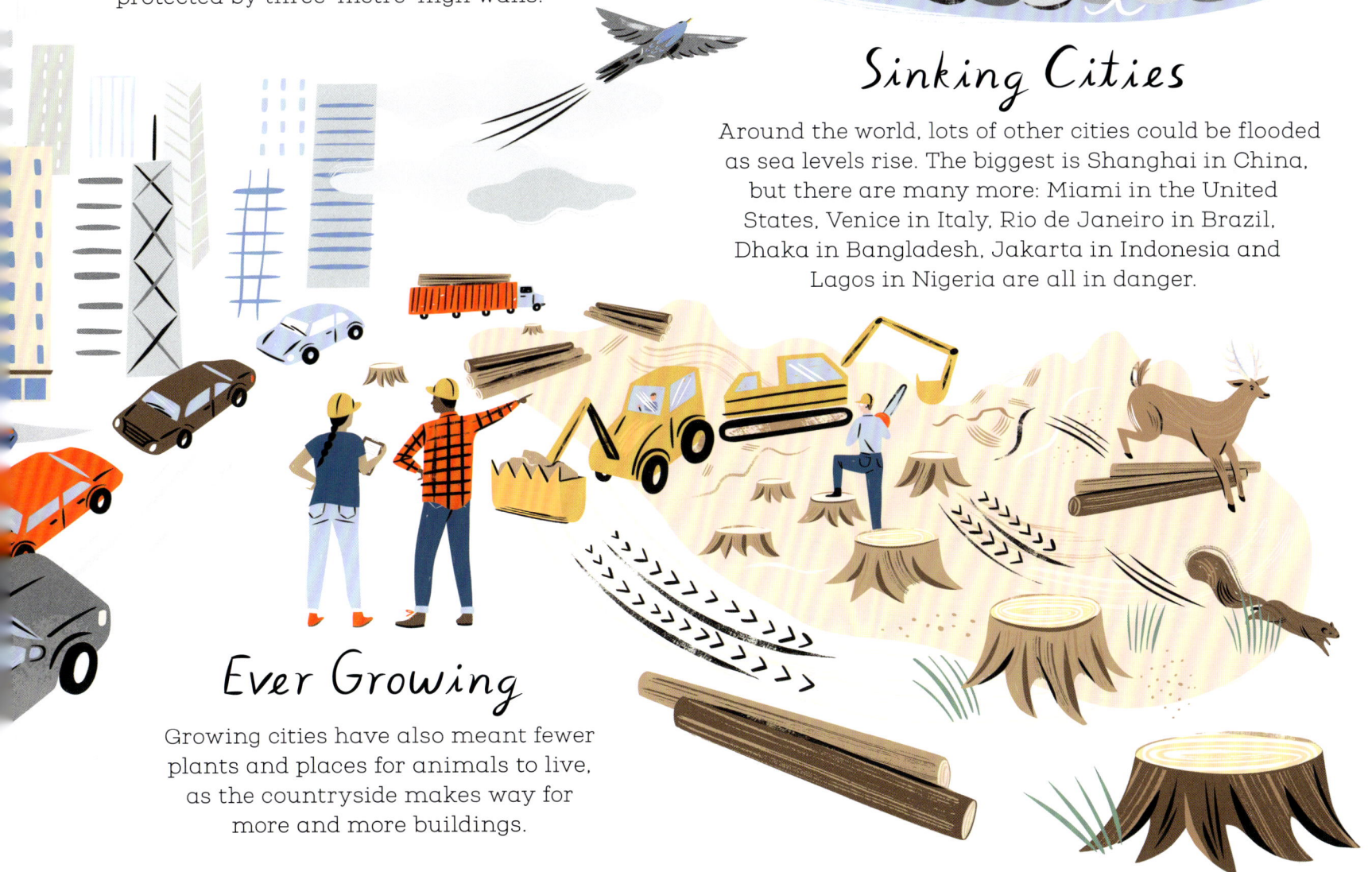

Ever Growing

Growing cities have also meant fewer plants and places for animals to live, as the countryside makes way for more and more buildings.

CITIES of TOMORROW

The good news is that people are thinking about ways to combat climate change, encourage plants and animals to thrive, and reduce air pollution.

Making Cities Green

Plants absorb carbon dioxide in the air, so the more of them there are the better. In southern China, the new Liuzhou Forest City will be covered in 40,000 trees and almost one million other plants. The city-island nation of Singapore, known as the 'Garden City', has a rule that all new buildings must include plant life in the form of vertical gardens and green roofs. And if you want to plant a tree in Los Angeles in the United States, the city will pay for it.

Renewable Energy

Instead of using fossil fuels, cities could use energy from the sun, water, wind or waves. Electricity generated from these energy sources doesn't add to carbon dioxide in the atmosphere. The cities of Aspen in Colorado and Burlington in Vermont in the United States, as well as the whole country of Iceland, are already powered completely by renewable electricity.

Getting Around

Building reliable, cheap and energy-efficient public transport means people will be less likely to make journeys by petrol- and diesel-fuelled cars. Electric cars will eventually take over from cars that burn fossil fuels. However, buses and trains still use much less fuel than people travelling in individual cars.

Smarter Cities

Cities can be made much more energy-efficient by using smart technology for buildings and public spaces – for example, installing streetlights that only light up when there are people around or escalators that only start moving once people step on board.

A Bright Future

Perhaps in the future city dwellers will get to school or work using solar-powered jetpacks or super-efficient smart pods. Perhaps animals will be allowed to make their homes on specially designed plant-covered buildings. With care and patience, the cities of tomorrow could help make our world a better, cleaner, greener and more inclusive place.

GLOSSARY

Abbasid   A dynasty of leaders who ruled the Islamic Empire from Baghdad between 750 and 1258.

activist   A person who campaigns publicly or works for an organisation to bring about social or political change.

alloy   A metal made by combining two or more types of metal.

altar   A holy table in a temple or church.

amulet   A small object or piece of jewellery carried to offer protection from evil or danger and to bring good luck.

Anglo-Saxons   The people who lived in England from the fifth century until the Norman Conquest in 1066.

apprentice   Someone who works for a skilled person in order to learn their trade.

aqueduct   A bridge or channel carrying water across country.

arena   A place where sport, entertainment and public events are held in front of spectators.

arsenal   A building where military equipment and weapons are stored or made.

bazaar   A market in an Indian or Middle-Eastern country.

Buddhism   A religion and philosophy founded by the teacher Siddartha Gautama, who is often known as the Buddha.

canal   A long, narrow waterway built to carry water from one place to another or for boats to travel along.

catacomb   An ancient underground cemetery with passageways and rooms where people were buried.

citizen   A person who lives in a town, city or country.

city state   A city that, along with the area around it, forms an independent nation with its own government.

civil war   A war between different groups of people living in the same country.

class   A system where society is divided into groups according to social status.

Cold War   A period of hostility between the Western powers (including the United Kingdom and the United States) and countries of the Soviet Union.

colony   A country or area that is controlled by another country; people who come to live there from the controlling country are known as colonists.

convict   Someone who is in prison having been found guilty of a crime.

cosmopolitan   A cosmopolitan city is home to people from many different countries and cultures.

democracy   A system of government in which people vote in elections to choose their own leaders.

dynasty   A line of rulers from the same family.

ecological   Involved with or concerning ecology, which is the relation of different forms of life to one another and their environment.

ecosystem   All the plants and animals that live in a particular area and the relationship between them and their environment.

embalm   To preserve a dead body using special chemicals.

empire   A number of individual nations that are controlled by the government or ruler of a single country.

flagship   The most important of a group of things owned by an organisation or company.

floodplain   A flat area beside a river that is made up of sediment deposited by the river when it floods.

gladiator   A person, especially in the Roman Empire, who fought wild animals or other gladiators to entertain an audience.

immigrant   A person who comes from one country to live in another.

indigenous   A person, plant or object that originates in a particular place; native.

informant   Someone who gives another person information.

LGBT+   Lesbian, gay, bisexual, transgender, plus any other sexual and gender identities.

Mass   A Christian church ceremony to remember the last meal of Jesus Christ.

mead   An alcoholic drink made from honey and water.

Middle East   The land to the south and east of the Mediterranean Sea, including Iran, Egypt and other parts of North Africa and southwestern Asia.

monarch   A king, queen, emperor or empress.

monastery   A religious community of monks, also the place where they live and worship.

mourning   Showing deep sadness, usually after someone's death but also to indicate the loss of something precious.

natural resources   Materials that exist in the natural environment and that can be made use of by people.

republic   A state where power is held by elected representatives of the people.

revolution   When a large group of people overthrow the existing government or monarchy of a country by force and install a new system of government.

rights   Things that every member of society is morally allowed to have, such as freedom and equality.

ritual   A religious ceremony in which a series of actions are performed in a set order.

sacrifice   The ceremonial killing of an animal or person to please a god.

salary   The money a worker is paid by their employer.

Second World War   (1939–45) The war fought between the Axis Powers (Germany, Italy and Japan) and the Allied Powers (France, Great Britain, the United States and Russia), partly in continuation of the problems of the First World War. The Allies eventually won the war. Around 50 million people were killed.

serf   A person who worked on the land and had to obey the owner of that land.

settler   A person who goes to live in a new country.

shrine   A place of worship connected to a particular god, holy person or object.

slum   An area of a city where very poor people live, with bad housing and crowded and unhealthy living conditions.

soup kitchen   A place that serves free food to homeless or very poor people.

Soviet Union   Officially called the Union of Soviet Socialist Republics (USSR), this was a political union of several countries and states governed from Russia.

smallpox   An infectious disease that caused the death of many people over centuries but has now been controlled by vaccination.

start-up company   A small business that has recently been set up.

state   The government of a country; alternatively, one of several smaller areas into which a larger country is divided.

stock exchange   A place where stocks and shares are sold. Shares are the small parts into which large companies can be divided then bought and sold to make money.

strike   A protest by workers who refuse to work in an attempt to get better pay or conditions.

tax   Money paid by people to the government.

tenement   A large, old building divided into flats.

INDEX

Acknowledgements

Thank you to Kate Wilson, Rachel Kellehar, Holly Phillips, Tina García, Elizabeth Jenner, Tegen Evans and Sophie Banks at Nosy Crow for making the book happen, and to Miranda Baker for her excellent proofread. Thanks also to the knowledgeable and helpful curators and editorial team at the British Museum for all their hard work and brilliant ideas, especially Bethany Holmes and Claudia Bloch, and also to Simone Felton from the San Francisco Historical Society. You have all been wonderful.